Osca
Moretti
Stanguellini

ISBN 1 84155 627 0

Published by
CP PRESS
PO BOX 2795
HOCKLEY, ESSEX. SS5 4BY

First published October 2005

Osca

Contents

LET'S GO TO LE MANS

by Andy Heywood

ANOTHER LEAP OF FAITH confronted Francesco Giardini as he once again rounded Tertre Rouge and plunged from the relative light of the complex into the mesmerising darkness of Mulsanne. The shadows of trees that lined the route formed his only reference and while deep into the distance glinted the hue of red tail lights, he knew that he could not give chase.

The little 1,500 cc engine sang with all the brilliance of its Bolognese creators yet,

as always, he would have to restrain its willingness to reach an ultimate crescendo that could lead to its destruction. A glance down through the spokes of the steering wheel to the rev counter showed 6,000rpm and aurally he agreed. There were still another 12 hours to go after all. With the experience of familiarity, he gently tempered the pressure of his right foot on the sensitive throttle and delicately flexed his jaded muscles.

This would be nearly two minutes of relative relaxation. He calculated he speed to be around 200km/h and slumped low in the aluminium-tubbed seat to further encourage the passage air over the Plexiglass windscreen. With

deft movements of his fingertips, he felt every undulation of the road. The once communicative steering was at this speed unnervingly light, and piloting the small car down this wide tree-lined road became akin to threading the eye of a needle. Time now to glance at the other gauges. Water temperature was low in the cool night air and so he reached under the metal tonneau to pull halfway out the lever that controlled the slats for the radiator blind. Oil pressure was a massive 6 bar, normal though, and necessary to lubricate those two delicate camshafts and their finger followers. The rhythmic lullaby of the engine was now working at his fading stamina with

Osca

This Mt4 was built by Carrozzeria Fratelli Morelli of Ferrara. It's a small car with a big history

soporific effect and his mind wondered to thoughts of class victory for himself, for the honour it would bring to his hometown of Ferrara and to the Maserati brothers in nearby Bologna.

Oil pressure was a massive 6 bar, necessary to lubricate those two delicate camshafts

Flashes of light dancing energetically in the rear view mirror broke him from his lonely reverie and signalled forthcoming ▶

Osca

drama. Gently manipulating the car to the side of the track, he braced himself as the leaders came past. The clamorous combination of elements and OSCA delayed the acoustic arrival of the Gonzales-Trintignant Ferrari but when illuminated in the beam of the Marchal headlights, the sonic boom from the mighty 375 Plus was awesome and Giardini could but spectate from the best seat in the house. Moments later, a broader, basso tone followed as a D type Jaguar gave chase at approaching 180mph.

They had by now rounded the infamous kink, something that the OSCA could take flat out, and although he waited for the landmarks that signalled the braking area, the fairground illuminations of the leaders' brake lights ahead warned that now was the time for Giardini to pull himself up into command of the car and focus his mind on the difficult corners between here and the start of another lap.

The year was 1954, but it was not to be Giardini's, as although history does not record whether it was he or co-driver Peron, it does, however, record that after seeing the pit board at the end of the Mulsanne straight in the twenty-third hour which showed their OSCA, number 42, as leading the class, one or other of its drivers, struck by the excitement of potential honours, suffered a momentary lapse of concentration and as the French put it "depart le circuit".

The 1,500cc twin plug engine had been fitted in the car specifically for the 24-hour race, and back in Bologna it was substituted for the original single plug 1,100cc unit which the car had used for its first abortive competitive event, the 1954 Mille Miglia. As such, Giardini participated in more home-grown competitions throughout the rest of the '54 season, most notably gaining a second in class at the Coppa D'Oro Delle Dolomiti. At the end of the year the car was sold to Attilio Brandi of Florence who pressed it into further, successful competition during 1955, including first in class at the Giro Di Sicilia. In the meantime Giardini transferred his allegiance to Modena and to a Maserati A6GCS.

Both were to compete a year later in one of wettest Mille Miglias in the history of the race. While Giardini in the Maserati made a good start, the little OSCA with Brandi at the wheel was the only one of them to make the finish. Driving like a demon in the appalling conditions rewarded Brandi with a time of 14 hours 48 minutes. The Moss/Jenks record of the previous year was 10 hours 7 minutes in the 300 SLR. Good weather and three times as many horses make a lot of difference, so by comparison the diminutive OSCA's time is incredible.

Osca

Predictably, Brandi won first prize in the 1,100cc sports-racing category in the process.

The now two-year-old car went through somewhat of a barren patch. Brandi continued to campaign it in 1956 though with more retirement than success and moved on at the end of the year to another, newer OSCA. By 1958 the car had found its way to Sicily and in 1961, owned now by Mario Raimondo of Palermo, it was entered in that other great road race, the Targa Florio. Retirement from this event signalled the end of a tired and outdated racing car's international career and although Raimondo entered a number of national events throughout

1962, at the end of that year the car was put away and like many machines of that era, forgotten.

Fast forward to 1989 and in the depths of a Sicilian underground car park, a stone's throw from the Piccolo Madonie circuit, photographs of an ugly and hopelessly tatty red car are taken. Two and a half decades of unsympathetic storage rendered it almost unrecognisable but lifting the bonnet and brushing away the corrosion on the magnesium cam cover revealed four letters - OSCA. Scraping away the accumulated layers of paint on the chassis and a number became visible - 1143. Giardini's car, the 1954 works entry at Le Mans, is back in the land of the living.

ABOVE OSCA MT4 chassis number 1143 received an extensive restoration following its 25 years sojourn in a Sicilian underground car park

Taking their leave of the Trident, the three surviving Maserati brothers formed the Officine Specializate Costruzione Automobili concern in the San Lazzaro district of Bologna in 1947 in order to pursue their first love – motor racing. The MT4 series of cars was the first result of this new endeavour and drew heavily on experiences gained through the years at Maserati. The first series MT4s used a tubular chassis and a relatively crude looking cigar-shaped body with cycle ▶

Osca

wings. Powered by a new four-cylinder engine of 1,100cc and with only a single overhead camshaft, they developed 72bhp at 6,000rpm. A lowly output maybe, but weighing only 480kgs meant that the power to weight ratio made them useful, controllable and popular. Constant evolution of the engine meant that by 1954 the 1,100 cc unit had become a twin cam (called 2AD) with 92bhp at 6,600 rpm.

Coachwork had also become more sophisticated with pretty barchetta bodies featuring the handiwork sometimes of Frua, but mostly the little known Carrozzeria Fratelli Morelli of Ferrara. As per '50s Italian sports-racing cars in general, no two bodies were alike and modifications could be made chassis by chassis depending on the use for which the car was destined. For instance, this car features larger headlights than some,

specifically for Le Mans. In order to comply with the enormous variety of class requirements, the Maserati brothers also produced an equally large number of engine sizes. The twin cam 2AD could be specified in 1,350cc form using the same aluminium block, and from 1953 an iron block version with twin spark ignition was offered in both 1,450cc and 1,500cc forms, the latter's output reaching 120bhp.

The legacy which the brothers left behind at Maserati must have been vast, as the parallels in terms of evolution and engineering solutions between the products of these two companies during the period are astounding. No surprise then that in the '80s, as the products of Maserati started to become recognised by the classic car enthusiast, so too did their diminutive relations.

Removed from its Sicilian catacomb, the now valuable 1143 began a new life.

TOP Andy Heywood at the wheel a few days before the car was dispatched to Brescia where owner Alexander Fyshe drove it in the 2001 Mille Miglia

Following a return to Bologna for restoration under the guidance of ex-OSCA employees, in 1998 it became part of the Italian car collection of Alexander Fyshe in the UK. As befits a car that weighs 530kgs, there is not much to it. Spindly door frames are covered with just a single aluminium skin and the interior is just an open area beneath the body. Aluminium sheet screwed over the chassis protects the driver from the road, but on top even the smallest will be head and shoulders above the windscreen. However, the driving position is comfortable, though not, I would suggest, in the 24-hour sense. With only the most basic of controls available,

Osca

ergonomics do not enter the equation. Many of these were sourced from production cars so those who are au fait with Fiat Topolinos may feel at home.

In 1998 1143 became part of the Italian car collection of Alexander Fyshe in the UK

To start, insert ignition key and push to switch on ignition. Pump the throttle a few times and then grope under the dashboard on the passenger side for the lever to engage the starter motor. With a bad tempered cough and splutter the engine bursts into life and must be coaxed into idling. For such a small car it is incredibly loud, with the twin exhaust pipes exiting ahead of the rear wheel just under the driver's left ear! The engine is very smooth and there is no torque reaction when blipped. Maybe this is because there is very little torque, something that becomes apparent when pulling away. To get the car off the line requires bags of revs if clutch slip is to be avoided. Once on the move and with the revs rising, the noise builds even further and the driver's hand falls naturally to the stubby gear lever to try for second. It is a four-speed gearbox with synchromesh only on third and top, and in order not to lose all momentum and let the engine bog

down, a clean and forceful change into second is necessary. Running at slow speeds requires a lot of concentration and finesse, as the suspension is hard and the throttle ultra sensitive as it is but a short rod journey between foot pedal and carburettor butterflies. Any rough road will bounce your foot around on the pedal with embarrassing results.

Once out on the open road things become easier. The second act in the gearbox repertoire is much more fluid and although the wind begins to buffet and the noise just keeps growing, the engine now starts to respond more readily. Below 2,500rpm it is nothing more than irritated. From that point to 3,500rpm, it feels like

BELOW The low windscreen offers little protection against the elements. The goggles are not for show - you can't see to drive without them

an old car that could potter along all day but never set the world on fire, yet persevere upwards and suddenly the lobes climb back on to the camshafts, all those grumpy hydrocarbons fall into line and the little bird sings loudly.

It feels like a stressed-out Lotus Seven. Dainty steering. Hard, yet compliant suspension. Massively powerful brakes, drums all round with the superbly solid pedal necessary for heel and toe gearchanges, yet it only really happens at a stratospheric level of decibels and engine revolutions. When it does, it is fast and furious.

It is a heady and fatiguing experience to drive the car only a short distance and the knowledge that it competed in all those long distance races not only fills one with a sense of history but of awe for the drivers. It is no wonder that the car receives such a rapturous welcome in Ferrara on the first night of Mille Miglia retrospectives. Giardini's people still support their hero's car. And, of course, the body was also made there. On last year's event, while in the parc ferme during the small hours of the morning, an old man ambled over and pointed to the Fratelli Morelli script on the front wing. "My name is Morelli," he said, "I made this car." ∎

Osca

Osca 1500 Bertone

Osca

A MASERATI WITHOUT THE NAME

In 1938, the Maserati brothers sold out to the Orsi's, but in 1947 they re-emerged to build OSCAs. These never, however, captured the 'Maserati' flavour

Above left: Ernesto Maserati at the wheel of the first OSCA, the 1948 1100 cc MT 4

Above: Serafini guides the 1342 cc MT 4 OSCA on its way in the 1949 Circuito del Garda

Left: the first OSCA, seen this time with bodywork in place

Right above: Ernesto Maserati again. This time he stands next to the company's 1952 Formula Two contender

Right below: the 60° V12 engine as used in the 1951 Grand Prix car, seen *opposite page, bottom*

THE STORY OF OSCA begins over half a century before the birth of the marque. An Italian engine driver's six sons, the Maserati brothers, became passionately involved with motor cars. They were Carlo, Bindo, Alfieri, Mario, Ettore and Ernesto. Carlo, the eldest, was chief test driver for Fiat before joining Bianchi, for whom he also raced. He died at the age of 30, by that time running the Junior car firm and being involved with the design and construction of aero engines.

Mario preferred a paintbrush to a spanner and became an artist. Alfieri began to race, while Bindo became test driver for Isotta Fraschini. After World War I, Officine Alfieri Maserati, which had started as a repair shop some years before, began to grow. Alfieri, Bindo and Ettore (who had been involved with Alfieri in the construction of a racing car in Argentina before the war) were joined by the youngest brother Ernesto (a wartime pilot) and the four designed, built and prepared racing cars. For two years they developed Isotta Fraschini machinery, then Diattos and finally, in 1926, cars which bore their own name, Maseratis.

The brothers lived a hand-to-mouth existence. They were far happier building the cars in the little factory at Bologna than attending to the administration. In 1932 they suffered their first major setback when their company's founder and head, Alfieri Maserati, died; he had never fully recovered from an operation following a crash in the Targa Florio some years earlier. Bindo, Ettore and Ernesto decided to carry on, the last-named now head of the firm which had built and sold some highly successful racing cars. The next crisis came in 1937. Sales dropped as the brothers' cars were not as competitive as before, one of the reasons being the domination of the German Mercedes-Benz and Auto Union teams in Grands

Osca

Right: Luigi Fagioli gets an enthusiastic send-off in his 1100 cc car on the 1950 Mille Miglia

Above: the 1500 cc OSCA record car, run at Utah in 1955

Prix. In financial difficulties, they sold out to two wealthy industrialists from Modena, Adolfo Orsi and his son Omer. The Maseratis were retained on a 10-year contract and supervised the design and development of new models. In the early post-war years Maserati once more became one of the most prolific racing car manufacturers.

In 1947, their contract to the Orsis expired, Bino, Ettore and Ernesto Maserati left Modena to return to Bologna where, with the minimum of capital, they established a new company in a portion of their old, pre-1937 factory. It was known as OSCA (Officine Specializzate Costruzioni Automobili Fratelli Maserati); the brothers had been forbidden to use their own name by the Orsis. The intention was to revive the pre-Orsi days at Maserati by designing and building racing cars for the private owner. The three brothers— who did not drink, smoke or visit the theatre or cinema, such was their devotion to motor racing— started work with one lathe, one vertical drill, one shaper and one milling machine. The drawing office was Ernesto's bedroom. Ernesto was officially the development engineer, Ettore the tooling-up engineer and Bindo the plant manager.

In 1948 their first machine appeared, an 1100 cc sports car which was also raced with success in Formula Two. In Naples, Luigi Villoresi drove the car in Formula Two guise to victory ahead of such notable opposition as Raymond Sommer (Ferrari) and Alberto Ascari (Maserati). Onlookers marvelled at the high standard of workmanship of the OSCA. The engine was a square (equal bore and stroke) four cylinder with a capacity of 1089 cc. Its specification included a chain-driven single overhead camshaft, a light alloy cylinder head and a fully-balanced five-bearing crankshaft. Two horizontal Weber carburettors were employed and a power output of 80 bhp at 6000 rpm quoted. The chassis frame comprised basically two large-diameter tubes braced by cross-members, a ladder-type arrangement that was the hallmark of the Maserati brothers. Front suspension was by unequal length wishbones,

Osca

torsion bars and dampers, while at the rear was found a rigid axle in a light alloy casing sprung by half-elliptics.

The same basic sports car design remained in production for years to come, with engines ranging in size from 750 cc to 1½ litres becoming available. But the Maseratis yearned to re-enter Grand Prix racing and in 1951 the Siamese prince B. Bira commissioned them to design and build a 4½-litre V12 engine to install in his Maserati 4CLT/48 chassis. By this time the 1½-litre supercharged engine of the Maserati was out-classed in Formula One and Bira hoped a more powerful engine—330 bhp at 7000 rpm was quoted for the 60-degree V12 engine of 78 mm by 78 mm, 4472 cc—would once more make the car competitive.

The OSCA's début was at Goodwood on Easter Monday. 'Bira' won the Richmond Trophy Formula One race and finished third in the Chichester Cup, also breaking the course lap record at 90.35 mph. At San Remo the radiator was damaged in a collision and after finishing fourth at Bordeaux Bira was third in his heat at Silverstone; the final was curtailed owing to a downpour. At the Whitsun Goodwood meeting the OSCA won its heat, but in the final dropped out with

Top left: Colin Davis with an OSCA Junior in the 1960 Pescara GP

Top right: Colin Davis again, this time with the 1958 750 cc Le Mans car

Above: a rare example of a four-cylinder 1500 cc OSCA, now in the San Martino museum

oil pump failure after raising the lap record to 92.12 mph.

A ski-ing accident prevented Bira from racing again until October, but a complete Formula One OSCA was on the grid for the Italian Grand Prix at Monza in September. Its chassis was of the familiar tubular ladder-frame construction, while the suspension was by unequal length wishbones plus coil springs and an anti-roll bar at the front and by means of a de Dion tube located laterally by a Panhard rod at the rear. Driven by Franco Rol, it finished ninth and last, lapped 13 times by Ascari's winning Ferrari. The OSCA was plainly overweight and under-powered and only appeared again after conversion to a sports car.

Following the success of converted sports cars in Formula Two, new six-cylinder 2-litre single-seaters appeared in 1952 and 1953 driven by Elie Bayol and Louis Chiron. The engine, a 1987 cc unit with a bore and stroke of 76 mm by 73 mm, featured twin overhead camshafts and developed 160 bhp at 6500 rpm. Chiron won at Aix-les-Bains and finished second at Syracuse and Sables d'Olonne, while Bayol was second at Albi. At this time the Maseratis collaborated with the French Gordini firm; Gordini at one time considered

Osca

Above: a 1960 1000 cc car seen at Vallelunga

Above right: the 2000 cc OSCA sports car of 1960; this car's four-cylinder engine featured a desmodromic valve system

Right: the Artom collection now has possession of this four-cylinder 1500 cc car

building a Formula One car using the 4½-litre V12 engine, while it was no coincidence that both OSCA's and Gordini's new Formula Two engines were originally going to be V8s but instead proved to be 'sixes'.

OSCA's chief successes came in sports car racing, especially in the rugged Italian road races such as the Mille Miglia and Targa Florio. From the original 1089 cc engine were evolved the 1342 cc (75 mm by 76 mm) model and the 1453 cc (78 mm by 76 mm) version. It was in a 1½-litre OSCA, owned by the American Briggs Cunningham, that Stirling Moss and Bill Lloyd took a sensational, if brakeless, victory in the 1954 Sebring 12-hours in Florida. Their diminutive machine vanquished cars with many times its engine capacity. This success resulted in a host of enquiries from the United States and a new factory was opened in 1955 four miles south-east of Bologna at San Lazzaro di Savena.

By 1958 production had reached between 20 and 30 cars a year, all cars being handbuilt by the workforce of 40. One of the few items supplied by an outside concern was the bodywork. Three models were available, all sports cars, for the 750, 1100 and 1500 cc sports car classes. A development of the original engine

of 10 years before, the Tipo 187 748 cc unit developed 70 bhp; the Tipo 273 1092 cc engine gave 95 bhp and the Tipo 372 1491 cc over 135 bhp. All three featured two twin-choke Weber carburettors which fed the mixture into hemispherical combustion chambers with central Marelli plugs and two valves per cylinder. The twin overhead camshafts were driven by gears and a short chain.

Above: the 1600 cc, 100 bhp OSCA GTS of 1962; various coachbuilders made bodies for this car, including Zagato and Touring

14

Osca

An experimental desmodromic valve 1490cc engine was seen from time to time in sports car racing and the 1½-litre Formula Two of the late 1950s. It performed well, and reliably, but as there was no real power advantage gained in having mechanically rather than spring-closed valves the project was shelved. OSCA had, of course, to consider the service aspect—many of their customers were in the United States—and, of course, cost.

Towards the end of 1959 a new category opened the way for more OSCA sales. This was Formula Junior, a new single-seater class intended as a cheap introduction to motor racing for new drivers. Engines of 1 litre or 1100cc had to be derived from production units. OSCA's answer was a front-engined machine of their usual ladder-frame construction. Front suspension was by unequal length wishbones and coil spring/damper units and a live axle was sprung by vertical coil springs at the rear. Power came from an OSCA-modified Fiat 1100 engine which developed a healthy 78 bhp at 7500 rpm. Works driver Colin Davies (a Briton who lived in Italy and the son of pre-war Bentley exponent and journalist S. C. H. Davis) found plenty of success in Italian races in 1960, winning a so-called World Championship for Formula Junior cars run by an Italian magazine. But the writing was on the wall. Rear-engined, independently-suspended British machinery quickly got a stranglehold in Formula Junior and by 1961 the OSCAs were also-rans on the race tracks.

OSCA produced a 2-litre sports car featuring a four-cylinder engine of 88mm by 81.5mm (1995cc) which produced 175 bhp at 6500 rpm, but lack of funds prevented its proper development. In 1960 the 750cc sports car had a reworked engine, the Tipo 187N; it had a shorter stroke (64mm by 58mm), a completely revised cylinder head and a power output raised to 75 bhp at 7700 rpm. A desmodromic-valve 1100cc engine was also made available to United States customers, while the 1½-litre engine found its way into Formula One cars designed and built by former OSCA customer Alessandro de Tomaso, an Argentinian living in Italy, but they lacked sufficient power. Work progressed on a completely new Formula One engine design under the direction of Fabio Taglioni, of Ducati motorcycle fame, but this V8 (rumoured to be air-cooled and with desmodromic valve gear) never saw the light of day and neither did OSCA's proposed spaceframe chassis (at last a rear-engined design).

Into the 1960s OSCA concentrated on the production of a series of Grand Touring cars. The reason for this step dates back to 1959 when Fiat asked to use the OSCA twin-cam sports car engine in their Farina-bodied 1200 model. Fiat built the engine in Turin, increasing the engine capacity to 1568cc (80mm by 78mm) and detuning it to produce 100 bhp at 6000 rpm. In turn, the Maserati brothers used the Fiat-produced engine (in more potent form) in cars of their own featuring bodywork by such stylists as Touring, Fissore, Boneschi and Zagato, the last-named producing a sporting coupé. Some OSCAs—notably the Zagato-bodied GTS with a 140 bhp engine—were raced, but no noteworthy successes were recorded on any of the world's circuits.

In 1963 OSCA became part of the MV Agusta concern, a company specialising in the construction of helicopters. Its boss, Count Dominico Agusta, built and raced high-performance motor cycles as a hobby and there was speculation that with the acquisition of OSCA he might be tempted to challenge fellow Italian Enzo Ferrari by building a Grand Prix car. As it was to transpire, this was not the case. OSCA GT models continued to be built for some time, while the ageing Maserati brothers experimented with various projects, but eventually production ceased and OSCA became part of motoring history like so many others before them.

MK

Above: Prince Bira's 4½-litre Grand Prix car of 1951; as can be seen, the car is finished in the splendid colours of the Siamese Prince

OSCA

Peter Collins reviews the history of OSCA whose 50th anniversary was celebrated at the Genova Autostory this year

Above: A 1963 Tipo 1600SP. This car is considered to be the last serious competition OSCA built, but never raced. It was reputed to have a six-speed gearbox, power output was 145bhp.

Above: A 1957 Tipo S-187. Its 750cc engine produced 70bhp at 7,500rpm. A similar car was driven to a class win at Le Mans by De Tomaso Right: Front view of the Tipo 1600SP.

Revenge - doesn't that conjure up images of Machiavelli and the Duchess of Malfi? It has always been seen as a special ingredient in the history of Italian families and dynasties.

Orsini and Zagari use the word in the title of their book on OSCA to describe the goings-on at the latter's factory in Bologna during the '50s.

Firstly, what was OSCA? It was yet another Italian car constructor to use an acronym for its title, in this case the letters stood for Officine Specializate Costruzione Automobili (Specialised workshop for car construction). I've often fondly imagined the management of companies from Fiat to Siata, from Alfa to ATS, sitting down after a few glasses of wine and dreaming the titles up between them, as not only did they have to mean something but they also had to sound right in their abbreviated form also.

Osca

Above: First OSCA to use alloy wheels was this Tipo FS-372 in 1958. Engine has desmodromic valve-gear. Right: A Fissore Coupé currently for sale in the UK.

OSCA was set up in Bologna on December 1st 1947 by the remaining Maserati brothers. Sadly, Alfieri had died in 1932, allegedly due to an incompetent operation, so the remaining brothers, Ernesto, Ettore and Bindo got on with the job of establishing the new company.

It could be argued that Maserati cars went through three incarnations: starting in the early '20s with Diattos, then becoming proper Maseratis, and finally becoming OSCAs. This is because Alfieri Maserati designed the 1925 Diatto eight-cylinder GP car, but Diatto failed so Alfieri took the project over and thus created the first Maserati. The new company's activities majored heavily on racing cars, those few road cars that were produced were thinly disguised racers. This was to cause problems when later, in 1937, the brothers had to sell the company to the Orsi family, but agreed to stay on for a ten-year period as consultants. As soon as this was completed they went back to Bologna (the 'new' Maserati factory was now in Modena) and set up OSCA, only too pleased to be back on their own as the Orsis

had wanted to build road cars, which didn't interest the three brothers.

Their 'revenge' started. As they had done under the Trident, so they did with OSCA. Their minds were concentrated on producing competition cars and the first to appear, the MT4 (Maserati Tipo 4) was a cycle-winged open sportscar of 1,092cc with a tubular frame. The engine consisted of an iron block with alloy head and it developed 72bhp at 6,000rpm. The die had been cast. OSCA was to become a niche constructor of small capacity sportscars, hardly ever exceeding 2-litres.

Exceptions to this rule? In 1951, as a gesture to owners of supercharged Maserati GP cars of 1.5-litres, the brothers developed a 4.5-litre V12 for use in the new F1. Prince Bira took up the option but the car was slow. Meanwhile, Franco Rol drove a full OSCA 4.5-litre F1 car at the '51 Italian GP and at some races in '52 but again it was too slow and ended as a road

sportscar. Bira's car went to the Antipodes in the hopes that someone might buy it and apparently the story goes that it was left in Sydney as part payment for a 'debt' involving people who tend to work mainly at night. Somehow it found its way back to the UK and can now be seen at Tom Wheatcroft's Donington racing car museum. A third F1 car was built but not raced, and that also became a road sportscar.

Back, however, to the main story. It was August 15th 1948 before an OSCA took to the tracks and that was at Pescara, where Franco Comacchia suffered engine failure after leading the 1100 class. It all came right a month later at the Naples GP where Gigi

Osca

Owned by Alex Fyshe, this MT4 - 2AD (chassis 1143) was run at the Auto Italia Festival this year. It has a notable competition history that includes the 1954/56 Mille Miglias, and 1954 Le Mans.

Villoresi won outright. The brothers had arrived - again.

A second version - the MT4 1350 - still with cycle wings, appeared in 1949 with Serafini driving at the July Circuit of Garda races, but he retired. Neither sales nor results were stacking up as well as the brothers had hoped so a new engine, the 2AD (Due alberi di distribuzione or twin-cam) was developed and this was inserted into an updated MT4. Gone were the cycle wings, replaced with a contemporary all-enveloping body which at first swept downwards between the wheels on each side but eventually this area was filled in a la Ferrari 801.

Success followed quickly; Fagioli finished seventh overall and won the 1100 class in the April 1950 Mille Miglia and in September Bonetto and Sommer took a 1-2 at Monza in their 1100 MT4 - 2ADs, averaging over 150km/h into the bargain. Giulio Cabianca became a star performer, gaining six important class wins during the '51 season as well as numerous good placings. Overall OSCA had gained 21 wins from 39 starts.

These victories were all very well but the brothers still hankered after single-seater success and when the Grand Prix rules for

1952 were announced for 2-litre F2 cars they set to work and came up with a 1,987cc six cylinder car for Frenchman Elie Bayol. He finished second at Siracusa in '53 and Chiron was fifth at Silverstone in the second chassis constructed. Bayol then won at Aix-les-Bains. Finally, in 1960 Colin Davis won the Italian Formula Junior championship in an FJ OSCA with front engine, but this was the last monoposto from the company.

Throughout the '50s OSCAs kept to the forefront of European small-capacity sportscar racing and also had an enthusiastic following in the USA although the cars were never turned out in any great numbers from the factory. Considering the quality of their results it comes as a surprise to find that no more than 10 to 20 cars were built per year. The brothers were meticulous over detail, trouble is that sort of approach doesn't lead to a big profit at the

Above Left: A 72bhp MT4 1100, an example of a first series OSCA from 1949.
Above: A 1956 MT4 1500TN (Tipo Nuovo) with coil sprung rear suspension. Engine is 1,490cc and has 130bhp.

end of the day.

Meanwhile, the cars that had gone to the USA were racking up some good results in the hands of drivers of the calibre of Bob Said, Bill Spear and Briggs Cunningham. Perhaps the greatest OSCA result was in the '54 Sebring 12 Hour Race when Briggs had invited Stirling Moss to share his MT4 1450 with the former's brother-in-law. Stirling is reported to have described the car as "a real little jewel" and, after the failure of the Lancias, the Bolognese car was cajoled into winning the race overall. For most of the race it was brakeless so Moss and Lloyd threw the car sideways through all the corners to slow it down.

Back in Europe, the MT4 - 2AD featured here ran in the '54 Mille Miglia, followed by a third in class at the Eifelrennen at the Nurburgring, driven by owner Giardini. It also ran at Le Mans in the same year where it retired having been temporarily fitted with a 1500 motor.

At the end of the 1954 the Maserati brothers moved the business eight kilometres to a new factory at San Lazzaro di Savena and began to concentrate on the 1,500cc class. Here they were to come up against the Orsis' new Maserati, the 150S, as well as competition from Porsche. The new engine was of 1,490cc and it was designated "TN" - Tipo Nuovo.

The "-ini" factor intervened in 1956 when the Tipo 187 appeared with a 750cc engine to compete in this traditional small capacity Italian sportscar stronghold. Another of OSCA's famous results was achieved with one of these

Osca

Top: One of 128 very pretty Zagato-bodied Tipo 1600GTs.
Left: This 1956 Tipo S-950 is a one-off and won its class in the 1957 Mille Miglia. It also ran in the 1959 Sebring 12-hours and came fifth in class driven by Ricardo Rodriguez.

Auto Italia office cat is called Osca!

females, Maria Teresa de Filippis and Ada Pace.

During the late '50s and early '60s Alessandro de Tomaso was learning all about motor racing with a variety of OSCAs, the first of which were owned by his wife Isabel Haskell. When he started to turn out his own single-seaters a number of them were OSCA powered.

However, despite the best efforts of Scarfotti, Stanga and many others, the cottage industry that was still OSCA simply couldn't last. The very reason for their split with the Orsis - the brothers' decision not to be road car builders - was overturned in 1960 with the appearance of the 1600 GT. Utilising a twin-cam four-cylinder engine, 128 were constructed between 1960 and 1963 with bodies from Zagato, Fissore, Touring, the inevitable knife-edge example from Boneschi, and one from erstwhile coachwork supplier, Morelli. Modified Fiat 600s were also produced and a tie-up with Fiat meant that the perpetually under-capitalised company was able to see its name on the cam-covers of the engines in Fiat's contemporary cabriolet. Il Fratelli Maserati couldn't afford to do it, but a visit to Dante Giacosa in '57 paved the way for a deal where OSCA powered Fiats rolled off Mirafiori's production lines.

Alas, it was borrowed time; a final fling in '63 produced a neat 1600 racing coupe with six-speed gearbox, but this was hardly even tested and so, on August 4th the same year, the brothers sold out to Count Agusta of motorcycle fame. A blast from the past was introduced in the form of Giaochino Colombo who oversaw the construction of the 1700 Zagato, a road car with, horror of horrors, a Ford V4 engine. Under the circumstances it is surprising the company clung on until 1966.

OSCAs may have been small, but these cars were emphatically not toys. For nearly fifteen years the brothers had done their own thing - maybe they did get their revenge. ■

cars when Alessandro de Tomaso took one to a class win at Le Mans in 1958, defeating Lotus. The little undersquare twin-cam produced 70bhp and the designation '187' imitated Ferrari as that was the capacity of each cylinder. Similarly the Tipo FS 372 - Sport. With 372cc per cylinder it was introduced to bolster the fortunes of the venerable MT4, and desmodromic valve actuation was used in the hope that this would give the little cars an edge. Just to be sure that historians were kept on their toes, the Tipo S-950 came along for '56 and no, it didn't have a 3.8-litre motor, it really was 950cc although the car was used more for tests than serious competition.

What else? Well, we've missed out the 2000S which had a six-cylinder engine and was built during 1954 and 1955. A car of this capacity wasn't tried again until the four-cylinder 498 of '59/'60. The 187 was updated and redesignated 187N and the S - 273 of 1,100cc (those individual cylinders again) was introduced for '57. Wake up at the back, there will be a test later!

The point is, the brothers were in the business of building racing cars and the only way they knew how to do that with success was to keep coming up with new machines in order to keep the name OSCA competitive. That way people would continue to come to San Lazzaro with their bags of lire. The Maserati policy was still to concentrate on getting the detail right on each car, a policy a million miles from churning out production road cars. They were not afraid of change, though, incorporating disc brakes and alloy wheels as quickly as anyone, and they were helped by their cars being driven by many 'names' of the period, including two very quick

PRODUCTION HISTORY

TIPO	YEAR
MT4 1100	1948-9.
MT4 1350	1949-50
MT4 2AD 1100	1950-56.
1350	1951-53.
(F1car)Tipo G 4500	1951
(F2 car) 2000	1952-53
Tipo 2000S	1954-55
MT4 2AD 1450	1953-55
1500	1954-57
TN - 1500	1955-56
S - 1500	1957
FS -372/F2S	1957-59
S - 187	1956-58
S - 187N	1959-60
S - 950	1956
S - 273	1957-59
S - 498/DS	1959-60
SF 392	1960
F. Junior J.	1959-61
1600 GT	1960-63
1600 SP	1963
1700 GT	1965-66

Osca

OSCA 2500

by Francesco Gregori

The flowing lines of the new OSCA come from the drawing board of Ercole Spada, well known for his designs while at Zagato

An Italian-Japanese initiative brings together some famous names to produce a sensational new sportscar

Amazing what a difference even a decade can make. To me OSCA is little more than an obscure name from the fifties and sixties. Although I dimly remember it was involved in racing, it certainly does little to fire my imagination. But so much as breathe the word to an older enthusiast and the reactions polarise between misty eyed reminiscences about racing in the days when men were gentlemen and chivalry still played a role, to an outright passion as several hard-fought races are vividly recalled.

Fortunately for this generation of people, the plans to revive OSCA (Officina Specializzata Costruzione Automobili Fratelli Maserati) appear to be a serious attempt to create an Italian equivalent to TVR or Marcos - rather than a cynical exercise in resurrecting one of the wealth of defunct Italian marques solely for short-term commercial gain. The racing heritage shows through in the new OSCA 2500GT, which features a composite body over a tubular space frame steel and aluminium chassis.

The whole car appears well thought through, with attention to detail apparent throughout. Weight saving has been a key priority with the result that, despite being bigger that the acclaimed Lotus Elise (409cm long versus 373cm for the Elise), it tips the scales at a seriously flyweight 680kg. The most obvious external sign of this are the 16inch magnesium alloy wheels, which are among the lightest available commercially. Lightweight alloys are also used widely in the running gear and suspension (variable quadrilateral front and rear), with many components being specifically made to

Osca

Compact flat 4 Subaru engine unit allows the OSCA 2500GT to sit very low on the ground, indicating excellent handling potential. Headlight trims and the subtle double-bubble roof are typical Zagato styling features

order by specialist engineering outfits. These are the same high tech 'artisans' which service the racing infrastructure in Italy and whose roots often lie in the era that spawned the original OSCAs. So it comes as little surprise that assembly and finishing of the body will be by Touring Superleggera, the specialist bodyshop which produced the commended OSCA 1600GT in 1961.

Although more aggressive and extreme, the styling certainly harks back to the OSCAs of the period, particularly at the front where the faired-in headlights and air intake give a definite early 1960s feel. Again this should be of little surprise when one discovers that Ercole Spada, the famed Zagato designer who penned many memorable cars of the era, was coaxed back to design the 2500GT. Despite its retro touches, the bodywork is aerodynamically highly efficient, particularly around the cockpit and roof areas. Unlike many other overtly sporting machines (and in true racing style), the body has been designed to provide easy access to the car's chassis and mechanical components - with both front and rear sections easily removable for major work.

The cockpit itself is best described as snug and spartan. Climbing over the high and wide sills demands

Although more aggressive and extreme, the styling certainly harks back to the OSCAs of the period

some degree of physical dexterity (especially since the car is only 115cm tall) but, once inside and installed in the highly supportive bucket seats, the driver is faced with a wealth of instruments and switches. These have been purposefully designed to convey a racing feel and, after only some initial confusion, fall easily to hand in a way that encourages tactile exploration. The multi-adjustable wheel also helps to ensure that most drivers will find a comfortable seating position. The rest of the cabin is basically bare; for instance, the door pulls are simply a piece of steel wire. Similarly, storage space is noticeably absent, although a small oddments bin has been incorporated into each door trim. A neat touch is the inclusion of a small flexible light between the two seats, which can be used either for interior illumination or for map reading in true rally style. Windows are limited to a small wind-up section, whose primary purpose is more to enable payment of motorway tolls than to provide ventilation. Instead, that is taken care of by the standard fit air-conditioning; it makes you wonder what the weight could come down to if they really tried!

Just as the inside deliberately favours analogue instruments over digital, the mechanicals also actively shun any electronic intervention. With the exception of

the makers claim this car is aimed at the tr

OSCA 2500 GT

electronic fuel injection, there are no concessions made to modern driving devices. That means no ABS, no traction control, and no other electronic aids to stability or roadholding. The makers claim this car is aimed at the truly enthusiastic and knowledgeable driver who can handle and control a car through skill, rather than relying on computers to escape from trouble. In this respect the 2500GT does recapture the spirit of the late 1950s when, in order to travel quickly, drivers had to be able to 'dominate' their cars. Fortunately, outright performance in a straight line is less important than handling and the car's set-up provides ample driver feedback of what the chassis and wheels are doing, even during fast driving.

Surprisingly for such an overtly Italian car, power is provided by Subaru's 16-valve, 2,457cc four cylinder 'boxer' engine (EJ254), which is mid-mounted and drives the rear wheels. Although only naturally aspirated and currently tuned to produce a modest 187bhp (138kW), thanks to the car's light weight this is still sufficient to generate an impressive power to weight ratio. The management would not be drawn on the subject, but power freaks are already debating how comfortably Subaru's acclaimed turbo unit from the Impreza would fit and how much additional cooling would be needed. Similarly, the gearbox is also straight out of the Impreza parts bin, which suggests upgrading to a sequential gearbox should be straightforward enough. Now that combination would be a interesting idea!

Normally aspirated engine produces 187bhp mounted in the 680kg body. Installing the Impreza turbo unit would provide considerable tuning and competition potential

Returning to relative sanity, the 'new company appears to have realistic expectations for sales volumes. The initial plans call for some 300 cars to be made over a three year period, with production at the Varese factory rising to around three a week by the end of the first year. Prices have yet to be finalised, but the high labour content and custom made components suggest it will be around £50,000. The fact that the new OSCA is an out and out sportscar, with little concession to the rigours and practicalities of everyday driving, should be viewed as a virtue and not a handicap. If the quality of the concept car is reproduced in the production models, then finding buyers should not prove too demanding even at these prices. ∎

Osca

G.M.P. Automobili s.r.l.

Some fifty years after its first birth, the OSCA name is set to adorn the bonnet of a sporting car again. OSCA itself was a reincarnation, being the vehicle chosen by the Maserati brothers (Bindo, Ettore and Ernesto) to return to car building after having lost their original racing and granturismo operations. They started from a humble workshop in San Lazzaro, near Bologna, in 1947. Within a year they scored their first victory, with Luigi Villoresi taking a class win in the Sports category of the Naples Grand Prix with an '1100'. Further racing success followed, fuelled by the arrival of the 90bhp '1350' in 1949 and then the excellent '1100' twin cam.

Despite efforts to develop a competitive Formula 1 entry (with a normally aspirated 4,500cc V12), it was OSCA's dominance of the Sports class which is best remembered. Following the then standard business practice of "win on the weekend and sell during the week", OSCA also produced a number of attractive road cars. The best known of these is probably the 1600GT, which was first introduced in 1960. Sadly, financial difficulties followed and the Maserati brothers sold OSCA to MV Agusta in 1963, before it finally disappeared in 1966.

The OSCA renaissance is being orchestrated by GMP Automobili, a recently founded company which has brought in the skills of Ercole Spada and Mario Colucci. Other links with the past include Luca Zagato, son of the famed designer, with the Maserati family also represented by one of the sons. The Japanese connection is courtesy of Shozo Fujita, one of the main financial backers and a reason for the link with Subaru. ■

> **Prices have yet to be finalised, but the high labour content and custom made components suggest it will be around £50,000**

Interior fitments are striking and minimalist, a typical signature of Ercole Spada

OSCA 1500

a bit

In July 1957 Ernesto Maserati of OSCA approached Dottore Dante Giacosa, the then Head of Fiat Design and asked him if he would consider making a 1,500cc twin cam engine to an OSCA design. This was to enable OSCA to produce a roadgoing touring car which was a departure from building their better-known sports-racing cars. The Maserati brothers realised that there was no future in relying purely on competition machinery. Fortunately for Ernesto, Fiat were starting to develop a replacement for their uninspiring and underpowered 1200 Trasformabile. Giacosa agreed to OSCA's request on the basis that Fiat could also use the engine in their new convertible as an alternative to their own 1500 pushrod unit.

Fiat's new 1500 Convertible received a body designed and made by Pinin Farina that was fitted to the floorpan of the 1200 Gran

> **"If you want to see a pensioner crying, just ask me how much this car has cost me to date."**

Luce. The car was quite successful and between 1959 and 1966 over 32,000 were made, the total including 1200 Cabriolets, 1500 pushrod and twin cam OSCA-engined cars. All were cabriolets as catalogued and sold by Fiat, mainly in the USA and Europe. There was little chance of them being sold in the UK as the price of a left-hand drive 1500 cabriolet - as the OSCA-engined car was known - was only £100 less than a Jaguar XK150. But despite this, a few were imported and Huxford's of Porchester in Hampshire converted some to right-hand drive.

Now comes the intriguing bit. Who marketed the attractive 1500S Coupe shown here? Obviously Pinin Farina made the body, but owner Jim McClurg has yet to find any reference to a Coupe in Fiat's listings. In his book 'Fiat Sportscars', Graham Robson says that Pinin Farina sold the Coupe version through their own sales organisation. If so, was it as a Fiat or an OSCA? Jim McClurg would be delighted to know.

Jim bought ESJ 801 (formerly EPR 33D) in December 1996. It was described as a '1958 Maserati OSCA 1500 Coupe, complete but requires finishing'. Armed with the chassis and engine numbers, Jim quickly established the car was certainly not a genuine OSCA, but a Fiat/OSCA 1500S Coupe - a car fitted with

S Coupe . . .
of a mystery

an OSCA-designed twin cam engine made by Fiat. Jim liked the lines and overall size of the car so negotiated to buy it for a more realistic price than that originally asked.

Having bought the car Jim set about the 'finishing' work. Almost three years later he is nearly there! The first task was to undertake a right-hand drive conversion. Jim says, "She who must be obeyed said she wouldn't drive a left-hooker at any price". This proved to be fairly straightforward as the bodywork and chassis were already drilled for either option. Jim is not a slave to originality, so he decided to de-seam the front wings and do away with the trim strips that covered the external body

line along the car. The overriders were dispensed with as Jim considered the car to be over-adorned with brightwork. Reputedly prepared by a 'racing mechanic', the engine was installed and then removed immediately because it had no oil pressure. When it was stripped down Jim discovered that the main bearing shells had been fitted incorrectly, thus blocking off the oil flow to the cylinder head and camshafts. With the engine back in the car it "smoked like trouper". Embarrassed, Jim decided to live with the smoke and at least to drive the car for while. The car, however, had other plans. The steel petrol tank, which had been empty for 20 years, shed rust into the fuel line causing more stoppages. Acid cleaning of the tank didn't work so a new

tank was constructed from aluminium. Although the car was now running continuously it still smoked and began to jump out of third gear.

In 1999 Jim bit the bullet and decided to start all over again and rebuilt the engine completely, and also changed the four-speed gearbox to a five-speed 124 unit. Fingers crossed, Jim hopes that he now has a useable and very rare 1959 (date confirmed by Fiat) Fiat/OSCA Coupe. Jim, of fairly mature years, says "If you want to see a pensioner crying, just ask me how much this car has cost me to date." ■

Jim's car was spotted at AROC's 1999 Italian Car Picnic. 2000's event is at Kentwell Hall in Suffolk on July 16th. Ed

THE 1,100 c.c.

MASERATI-DESIGNED O.S.C.A

When, about three years ago, the remaining Maserati brothers saw the work of twenty years taken from them, by the purchase of not only their factory at Bologna but even the right to use their own name on any product that they might make, it would have been a brave man who would have forecast that in less than two years they would have produced another racing car, much less one that at times would prove superior to the products of their erstwhile organisation. Such, however, is the unvarnished truth, and it reflects great credit on the skill and courage of the three remaining Maserati brothers that, in the 1,100 c.c. O.S.C.A., they have brought forth something that can hold its own in any company under Formula Two.

Those of you who read my previous article dealing with the 1,500 c.c. car that the Maserati company are making for Formula Two, and which was the last car designed by the Maserati brothers before they lost control of their works, will find more than a family resemblance in the sectioned drawings that accompany this article on the O.S.C.A. In many ways it is a similar car, but with two less cylinders. For example, there is the same system of overhead camshaft operation by means of a triple chain with an adjustable tensioner. The disc-type crankshaft has a bearing between each crankpin throw, and the oil pump and distributor are driven by a double chain from the nose of the crankshaft. If by any chance this chain should break, the ignition system stops also, and thereby saves run bearings and expensive noises.

Now to the technical details. Bore and stroke are 70 m.m. and 71 m.m. respectively, giving a nicely square engine the piston speed of which is not excessive even at the peak revs of 5,500 per minute. Capacity is 1,094 c.c., each cylinder having a capacity of 273 c.c., which is a nice size to use with a compression ratio of 8 to 1 as the car can run on pump fuel. Horse power developed at peak revs is only 55 compared with the 150-odd of the Ferraris and Maseratis, but none the less the car gives a good account of itself against both these makes; its low weight of only nine cwt. complete must account for this.

Maximum speed is quoted at 102 m.p.h., but these cars have shown that they can exceed this figure by quite an appreciable margin. With piston speed only a bare 2,300 feet per minute at peak revs, the lasting powers of this motor should be quite something and it looks as though it would be a very hard engine to blow up as combined with the low piston speed goes very sturdy construction in all parts where stresses are high. Two Weber carburettors are fitted, fed by an electric pump, while ignition is effected by a coil and distributor. Force feed lubrication with a large capacity filter takes care of the bearings, and watercooling has the usual centrifugal pump which is mounted in line with the generator on the near side of the motor, the whole assembly driven by a double rubber belt from a pulley on the front of the crankshaft.

A study of the drawings will show what care has been taken to ensure that there is plenty of water between the cylinder bores and also round the valve seats; cooling water goes straight from the pump to the under side of the exhaust valves. So that the sparking plugs can be mounted centrally, the camshaft is slightly off centre in the cylinder head. This has meant that the inlet valves have had to be operated by means of short pushrods with roller cam followers. On the exhaust side, rocker arms bear direct on the cams; at the cost of a slight increase in the weight of the valve gear parts, a hemispherical combustion space with the sparking plug in its centre has been obtained.

Double valve springs are used; there is an individual exhaust port for each cylinder, but on the inlet side, the ports are siamised so that each carburettor serves two cylinders. Plain bearings are used for both mains and big ends, the gudgeons being lubricated by splash. The high compression pistons have steps cut in them so that they will not touch the valves if revs are taken a bit high for the valve gear at any time. The engine is mounted on rubber at three points, and great care has been taken to balance all reciprocating as well as rotating parts. 80 octane fuel is recommended, which is a pump fuel in Italy today—in Australia we have to make do with 74 octane or less, which seems to be another argument in favour of losing a war.

The gearbox, which has four forward speeds, is in unit with the engine, with a dry plate clutch interposed. From the gearbox, the drive goes through a balanced tail shaft with universal joints at either end to a semi floating rear axle, which is split on its centre line as have all Maserati-designed back axles since they first commenced manufacture in 1928. Rear suspension uses semi-elliptic leaf springs which take all torque and are shackled at their rear ends; they have piston type hydraulic shock absorbers. Front suspension is independent by two wishbones on either side with a coil spring between them. Hydraulic brakes with large ventilating scoops are fitted to all four wheels; the hand brake works on the transmission. Tyre size is 5.00 x 15, fitted to Rudge-Whitworth wire wheels with knock-off hub nuts. The electrical system is 12 volt, and the rear mounted tank has a capacity of 15 gallons. Mounted well forward, the steering box is on the near side of the car with its track rod carried in front of the suspension, just behind the radiator.

Wheelbase is only 91 inches; front track is 49 in., rear track 48 in. This makes for a very compact car which should be a delight on corners, but inclined to wander a bit on the straights. Ground clearance is under 6 inches so that it is as well to keep the car off unmade roads. The standard body is of the all-enveloping type, with a streamlined headrest on the tail behind the driver's seat. As can be seen from the drawings, the spare wheel is carried in the tail, and can be got at by tilting the two bucket seats forward. A light aero screen is mounted in front of the driver, but there is no protection for the passenger's face.

By using welded construction for the tubular steel chassis frame, the makers have got the maximum of strength with the minimum of weight. This frame has a number of sturdy cross members, and should be free from whip. The more one studies this car the more one can admire the genius of the team that designed it; it is doubtful if there is available anywhere to-day another 1,100 c.c. car of

Osca

such essentially simple and sturdy construction that can give the comfort and performance of the new O.S.C.A. After all, 100 m.p.h. on pump fuel with full road equipment from 1,100 c.c. takes a lot of beating, and I, for one, do not know of any similar car of that capacity being made either in Europe or America that can touch it. Just what its price is I do not know, but I hope that one day I may have the privilege of handling one somewhere.

As a development, and in order to bring its power development a bit nearer that of its rivals, a 1,350 c.c. O.S.C.A. is announced. This is exactly similar in appearance to the model described, except that the bore is 75 m.m. and the stroke 76 m.m., so keeping the square character of the engine. Revs are up to 6,000 a minute, but as against that the b.h.p. have gone up to 90. As the extra weight of the larger motor cannot be very much and the horsepower has been almost doubled, the 1,350 c.c. model must go extremely well and speeds in excess of 120 m.p.h. should not be out of its reach, even when carrying two people and the full equipment that goes with the car. With between 9 and 10 b.h.p. to each cwt., acceleration ought to be a bit out of this world also.

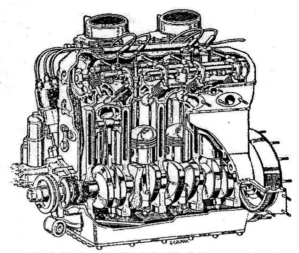

This drawing shows the rigid construction of the motor. Main points of interest are the five bearing crankshaft, good positioning of the valves, and the chain driven camshaft and auxiliaries.

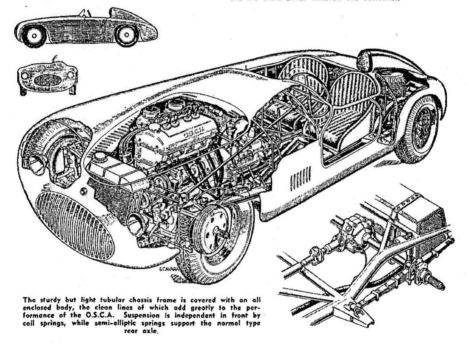

The sturdy but light tubular chassis frame is covered with an all enclosed body, the clean lines of which add greatly to the performance of the O.S.C.A. Suspension is independant in front by coil springs, while semi-elliptic springs support the normal type rear axle.

Alejandro de Tomaso puts the petite 1,100 through its paces at the Modena Autodromo

O. S. C. A. Spells

The Fratelli Maserati sold their

IF the automotive world can be said to have a fleeting, elusive Flying Dutchman, it must surely be the *desmo-dromic* O.S.C.A. engine. Ever since late 1956, when the Maserati brothers declared that they had dispensed with springs, manifestations of the new engine have been reported from Sebring to Rouen, the most insistent stories usually being filed by those who've just been trounced by the suspect car. The documented appearances are relatively few in number. First was in September of 1957 at Silverstone, fitted in a car which was end-over-ended in its heat. Not damaged, the desmo engine was transplanted to a sports framework and raced at Spa shortly thereafter.

Since these events the pressure of sports car production and the development of a *Gran Turismo* engine for Fiat had moved the brothers' mechanically-closed valves to the back of the bench, but the recent enthusiasm (and finance) of Alejandro and Isabelle de Tomaso has caused 'em to be dusted off and bolted to an engine of new dimensions mounted in a machine rife with features new to the O.S.C.A. organization. The resulting car is an intriguing *pot pourri* of the classical and scientific approaches to sports car design.

It's logical that the Maserati brothers should have been the first to follow Mercedes' lead and produce a practical modern mechanical system to replace the valve springs. As is well known, some very close clearances and precise adjustments are called for. These can either be designed-in by a concentrated engineering effort or individually built-in by expert, painstaking hand fitting. Daimler-Benz naturally chose the former route, while the *Officine Specializzate per la Costruzioni di Automobili*, with its intimate, feudal assemblage of artisans, elected an emphasis on execution rather than design. It works, and well, but frankly hasn't been so successfully exploited as was the case at Stuttgart. In view of the relative size of the coffers at Bologna it's most remarkable that the Italian interpretation was built at all.

For maximum utility, the desmodromic gear was first designed into the head for the 1,491 c.c. engine with its traditionally "square" 78 mm. × 78 mm. dimensions. With a probable eye on Porsche developments and on the current preoccupation of Lotus and Cooper with Grand Prix equipment, it was decided to fit this new car into Class G. The 1,350 c.c. block, a stepping stone from the original 1,100 c.c. O.S.C.A. to the Class F size, was pressed back into service to

provide a diminished bore diameter which, in connection with a much shorter stroke, reduced capacity to about 1,090 c.c. The exact dimensions haven't been released. Topping it off is the full 1,500 c.c. cylinder head, with appropriate valve, port and carburetter sizes. It should provide altogether exceptional breathing at the expense of a complete engine on the heavy side for a 1,100. You'll recall that O.S.C.A.'s most successful Class G contender to date was a 950 c.c. expansion of their very light 750 c.c. engine. The new car thus represents a full-circle turn in policy.

All the products of the Maserati brothers have been characterized by simple, reliable design and construction methods well-suited to the needs of the private owner—a tradition that began with their 1929 Maserati car, the first in European racing to have a detachable cylinder head. The light-alloy block casting of their O.S.C.A. of thirty years later is competently simple, its smooth flanks broken only by screw-in core plugs on the right, and by water and breather connections on the left. A flanged wet steel liner cylinder construction is used.

Ending conventionally at the crankshaft centre line, the bottom of the block comprises the upper half of the crankcase and carries webbing to support the five plain main bearings. Main caps are amply dimensioned and retained by two studs each. All O.S.C.A.'s for sale have plain bearings throughout the bottom end, but a further refinement has been carried out in this semi-factory machine. The rods have one-piece bottom ends for use with roller big-end bearings, fitting of the rods and bearings being allowed by an assembled five-piece crankshaft. No complex Hirth system for the Bologna boys. They just carve octagonal extensions on the rod journals which mate very tightly indeed with similar holes in the corresponding cheeks. The union is consummated by freezing the journals and heating the cheeks, then assembling with the rods and rollers in place. Such an arrangement depends entirely on skilled hand work both to machine the mating surfaces and to align the assembled crank properly. Understandably, such cranks won't soon be turned over to private owners.

A combination of plain main bearings with roller rod bearings is sensible from several standpoints. For one, it allows the use of the low-friction crank/rods assembly in an

Osca

Small car, ergo small truck

Maserati

Name but kept their Talent

unchanged conventional block. Since the supply of lubricating oil is invariably to the rods by way of the mains, this arrangement also facilitates an internal flow of oil to the rod rollers without the (admittedly effective) expedient of slinger rings. Roller mains and plain rod shells would of course be impractical from the lubrication standpoint.

Extraordinary in these days of oil/water heat exchangers, big oil reservoirs and multiple-scavenge-pump dry sump systems, this petite O.S.C.A. has a plain old non-cooled wet sump lubrication layout. A wide, deep cast-alloy oil sump flares out away from the crankcase bottom face to give as much finned cooling area on the bottom as possible, and also to hold as much oil as the proximity of the frame members will allow. A wire dipstick is inserted at the forward right-hand side, just aft of the single pressure oil pump. Bolted to the front of the timing chest right next to the oil pump, a small housing contains pressure-release and bypass valving and provides a mounting cap and stud for the angled replaceable-element oil filter.

Small pressure oil fittings are supplied on the sides of the block adjacent to the main bearing between cylinders three and four. A small tube from each carries oil to the centre outside of each cambox, from whence a gallery bathes the cam bearings and valve gear. Pressure is led to the dashboard gauge from a T-piece in the right-hand line. These very small pipes are the only external ducts in a very simple and hence reliable oil system. The use of a wet sump, with its limited capacity, also reflects O.S.C.A.'s confidence in the oil retaining ability of the design and assembly of their engine. Since their units have an absolute minimum of external joints and usually finish races as spotlessly as they start, it seems justified.

Now to the heart of this matter: the valve gear. Twin overhead camshafts are turned by a short set of three gears in the head which are powered by a roller chain from the crankshaft nose. Each cam is carried directly in the cylinder head casting by three plain bearings, their caps being retained by four studs each. Plenty of room is left in the widened camboxes for a desmodromic gear that closely resembles the Mercedes system in general layout.

Each valve is controlled by two cam lobes—one opening and one closing. Let's take the opening arrangement first. A conventional cam lobe is placed right over the end of the

valve stem end, and pushes the valve open by contacting a very small mushroom-type "tappet" which is *screwed* onto the end of the short-stemmed valve. To be precise the stem screws into a tapped hole in the shank of the tappet, and is locked in place by a tiny pin which is pressed through a hole in the side of the tappet shank to engage a keyway-like slot

Radiator opening is efficiently small, fully ducted. Frontal aspect is similar to Lotus

Lower part of tail section is vented to release heated air. Removal of top section of body is effected by removing hinge pin

Highly polished and machined upper wishbone is of aluminium and weighs but 10.6 ounces. Maserati-constructed dampers appear to have been an afterthought. The high-mounted anti-roll bar, dipped to miss the distributor can be seen above upper wishbone

Rigid rear axle is sprung on concentric coil spring/damper units and is located by two diagonal arms below and by a central arm above. Canvas straps limit rebound. Fuel from riveted tank is pumped forward by rear-mounted electric pump (bottom right)

along the valve stem. The threads being very fine, they assist in obtaining proper opening valve clearance.

Free to slide up and down along the tappet shank is a short tube with a flange at its upper end, and between this flange and the underside of the mushroom top a very short, stiff coil spring is compressed. Backtracking a bit, a small-diameter shaft runs the length of each cambox along the inner or spark plug side. From this shaft is pivoted a closing bell crank for each valve. One end of the crank reaches out and encircles, with an oval aperture, the sliding collar and flange on the tappet shank. Offset to left or right, depending on the valve, the other bell crank end is forked to accept a needle-mounted roller which rides against a large-diameter Mercedes-style closing cam lobe. Going in the other direction, the closing cam presses against the bell crank roller, causing the other end of the crank to lift up against the sliding flange and thus, through the short spring, against the underside of the tappet screwed to the valve stem. The adjacent opening and closing cam lobes are naturally contoured so that each complements the motion of the other, one backing off while the other rises, and vice versa.

As mentioned, all the valve closing cranks are pivoted from a common shaft for each cam, there being no neat independent adjustment for the pivot location of each crank as was the case in the Mercedes interpretation. This lack of a

Large diameter drums are fitted with vents for linting dust and water only. Recessed well into the wheels the massive cross finning look after heat dissipation. Back plates are fitted with a small air scoop

precise setting for total running clearance made the small springs along the stem necessary to ensure full seating of the valve. Keep in mind that these tiny springs do not actually themselves close the valves; they only keep the bell crank roller in constant and firm contact with the closing cam. Mercedes tried such springs in their valve gear at first but found them superfluous, thanks to the refinement of their adjusting system.

A detail worth mentioning is the application of pressure oil to the bell crank pivot shaft and finally to the opening cam and tappet by way of a spray hole in the bell crank. Although development is now at a relative standstill on this desmo gear, several details indicate the highly experimental nature of this head. The right-hand cam cover, for example, has a flange cast at its back end to accommodate a magneto or distributor if necessary (the left-hand cam turns the rev-counter cable). Just above the ports along the sides of the head are two-bolt access plates of the type usually employed by O.S.C.A. to support pivots for finger-type valve followers —possibly remnants of an earlier desmodromic try, or a pessimistic means of utilizing the casting if the mechanical closure failed to function. Eight core plugs down the centre of the head are an index to the complexity of the casting job, which included the provision of bosses for sixteen potential water offtake (or inlet) pipes, and wells for eight vertically-placed plugs for four cylinders.

Osca

Within the framework of the O.S.C.A. engine, experience at Bologna has been that the desmo gear greatly extends the maximum rev figure but has little effect on maximum power or the point at which it is reached. Were it to be applied in connection with direct injection and exceptionally high compression, as at Stuttgart, the results would have been different. As it stands it is certainly comforting to know that you are unlikely to bend a valve no matter how oblivious you are to the pleadings of the rev-counter.

A Marelli twin-coil distributor juts forward from the front of the cylinder head, where it is driven by the central cam train gear. Wires to the plugs are liberal in length and bound together at several points, while the coils are placed far away on the left side of the bulkhead. None of these latter features are known to favour trouble-free ignition, and it may not be coincidence that in trials the usable revs of this 1,100 c.c. engine have been limited to about 7,500 by erratic firing. Lodge plugs are used.

Conventional in most respects, the water cooling system is centred around a low-placed F.I.M. radiator, made in Bologna. For the first time a sports O.S.C.A. has a small separate canister in the hot water return line as a location for the pressurized filler cap. The eight offtake pipes on the intake side of the head are utilized, as is the back one on the exhaust side. Two small vee-belts from a crank pulley drive a generator slung along the left side of the engine, a shaft from the back of the generator being coupled to a water pump at the centre of the block. Its output is fed directly into the block at two points, adjacent to four crankcase breather outlets which are manifolded into two big plastic vent pipes.

Contrasting with most competition layouts, this water pump location delivers cool water to the already cool inlet side of the block and head. It wasn't always so, however. Until the 1957 season O.S.C.A.'s customarily had carburetters on the right and exhaust systems along the left-hand side, a configuration still used on the 750 c.c. cars. Before 1958 the works 1,500 c.c. cars, perhaps for drivers comfort, had the situation reversed, simplifying carb linkages as well. Since only the porting and valving were changed, all the auxiliary connections were in effect reversed.

In its final developments stage the desmodromic 1,500 O.S.C.A. moved up from 40 mm. Weber carbs to the more sophisticated 42 mm. size, one of the largest ever to be applied to a 1,500. When the head was bolted onto this 1,100 the same carbs were retained, certainly setting a record for Class G fours. Of course they're choked well down—to 34 mm.—but the potential is there. An electric fuel pump back by the riveted tank supplies a small frame-mounted fuel filter up front and then the two Webers through flexible hose and a T-piece fitting. The joints between carbs and head have limited flexibility, the carb weight being borne by three straps from the cam cover retaining capscrews. A modern scavenging layout is used for the exhaust piping, the last two pipes meeting in the customary pseudo-silencer and then reappearing to end just ahead of the rear tyre. Below the exhaust ports, cradled between the flared oil pan and a tabular side engine mount, is found the lightweight starter motor with its pull-wire actuation.

Non-webbed and fully enclosed, a two-piece bell housing shrouds the mechanically-actuated single-plate clutch and unites power production with torque multiplication. New for O.S.C.A. the long, but slim, gearbox contains five forward gear choices and has what was described to us as "motor cycle-type" gear engagement. Presumably they have abandoned the synchromesh previously used on third and fourth cogs and have reinstated a simple, rugged dog-clutch system for the top four ratios at least. In conjunction with small light gears this can produce extremely rapid changes, often faster than are possible with a baulking type of synchromesh. Gear changes, to the ear anyway, are indeed completed instantly.

At the gearbox tail-shaft, just below the handy lever extension, nestles an external-contracting band handbrake con-trolled by a non-locking lever on the right. Strictly for downhill starting grids like Spa. Hooke-type joints and a large-diameter tubular prop shaft link up to the rear axle, which like late Ferrari productions betrays a garish practicality: live! O.S.C.A.'s have used both spiral and straight bevel gearing in their split alloy centre sections, but since, as indicated by a neatly stamped tag, this one carries a tooth combination of 9×38 we can assume that they're the straight teeth giving a 4.22 ratio as used in the 1,500's. Employment of the big axle els dies in with the generally heavy-duty bottom end and drive line of this muscular 1,100. A ZF cam-type differential is also aboard.

Live-axle conservatism is reflected in a simple twin-tube frame which says, "So I don't look like an engineering textbook. I won't break!" And it won't. Incessant O.S.C.A. successes in chassis-breakers like the *Mille Miglia* and *Targa Florio* have signed and sealed that. In this case the two main members are round steel tubes about 3 in. in diameter, formed primarily by cutting and welding straight sections together. They begin at the front with two complex

Two large Weber carburetters complete with ram tubes are braced by straps to the cam cover hiding the desmodromic valves. Large plastic hoses are crankcase breather pipes. Hot water return pipe is fitted with a small canister which serves as a location for the pressurized filler cap

fabricated curved pillars for the suspension members, joined by a large tube low down and a smaller one at the top. They spread apart through the bulkhead and reach maximum separation at the seats, there being a 2-in. crossmember under the driver's thighs which supports the back of the gearbox and unites a pattern of angled and longitudinal central-bracing 2-in. tubes. A main 3-in. crossmember behind the seats ends the primary frame and forms a jumping-off place for rear suspension links and for the big tubes that arch up over the axle and are split into D-section members to support the riveted fuel tank and the battery.

As classic as the frame is the unequal-length wishbone front suspension. Accepting all the reactions of bucketed coil springs, dampers and anti-roll bar, the bottom arms are wide-based U-section forgings riding in metallic bushes for rigid location. In contrast the short top arms are profoundly

31

O.S.C.A. 1,100

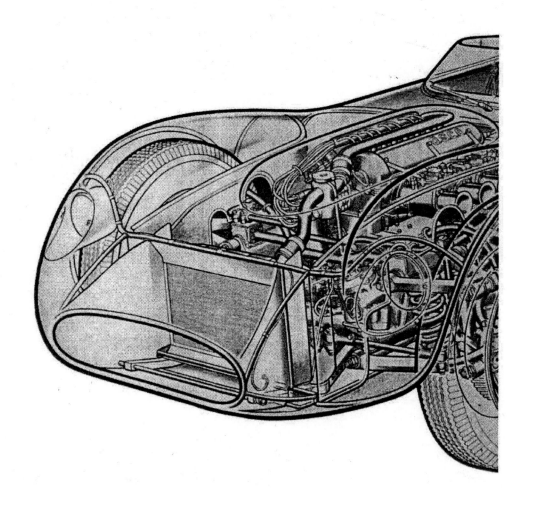

Osca

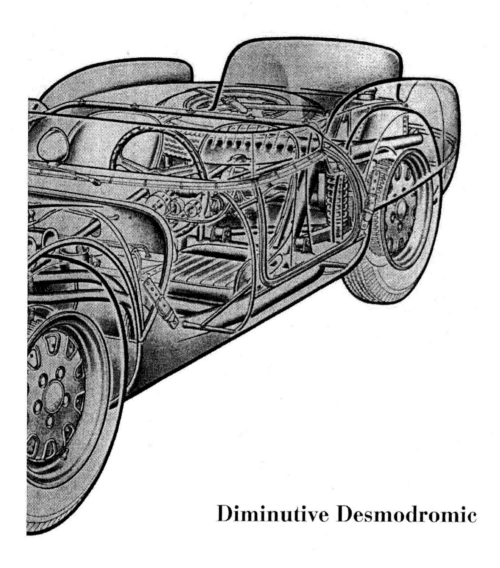

Diminutive Desmodromic

Rearward hinging tail section allows access to spare wheel and fuel tank and is limited in movement by a wire strand

daring by any standards, being machined out of aluminium blanks. They weigh a willowy 10.6 oz. apiece! The Maserati brothers also make their own tubular dampers, these very workmanlike units having two needle valve adjustments for internal fluid flow. They are not exceptionally well mounted, though, the travel being only about half that of the wheel for a given deflection—a disproportion which decreases the damper's effectiveness. Related criticism applies to the operating conditions of the coils and of the high-mounted anti-roll bar, which like the upper frame crossmember is dipped at its centre to circumvent the distributor.

Conventional steering joints embrace short king pins, below which are bolted the forward-facing steering arms. Simply, though not necessarily geometrically, these are joined by a two-piece track rod, the break occurring adjacent to the left-hand steering gearbox. Bolted into a fabricated niche in the frame and a considerable piece of machinery in its own right, this worm-based box actuates a forward-facing Pitman arm and takes commands from a chrome-plated steering column.

Good results with a distinctive layout are obtained by the O.S.C.A. location system for the light rear axle. Basic guidance is supplied by two fabricated box-section trailing arms which pivot at downward extensions from the steel axle housings. To provide lateral rigidity these arms are each braced to the frame crossmember by a small tubular strut with an angled rubber-bushed pivot at each end. An examination of this whole system will show that for one wheel to lift or for the car to roll the various rubber bushings in the members will be heavily stressed, imparting a degree of roll resistance but more importantly ensuring even firmer wheel control under such conditions. Putting it another way, if slop-free metal bushings replaced the rubber goods—the back end of this car could not roll at all. A parallelogram to resist drive and braking torques is completed by a single trailing arm from the top of the drive shaft tunnel to a pivot atop differential casing. Based on a 1-in. tube, the arm has deeply gusseted end fittings. Perfectly vertical coil springs surrounding O.S.C.A. tubular dampers are hung outboard of the frame and apply their forces to the boxed trailing arms just forward of the axle. Each bottom spring cup is

drilled for lightness and pivoted to its trailing arm. Axle travel is limited by canvas loops and rubber bump stops.

Brake mechanisms front and rear follow Maserati brothers' tradition in being of the conventional leading-trailing shoe type. The sturdy cast back plates have but a small screened air scoop and no air outlet, and are recessed well into the wheels to boot. Heat dissipation should however be well handled by massive new cross-finned brake drums which boast a large volume of aluminium bonded around their ferrous liners. Drum internal diameters are 10 in. in front and 9 in. in the rear. A pushrod and bell crank linkage from the pedal actuates the single master cylinder, placed in a decided hot spot between the left-hand frame member and the engine oil sump. An indicating plunger fluid reservoir is mounted on the bulkhead. Frequently seen on new O.S.C.A.'s of all sizes is a neat ten-spoke disc wheel, designed by Ernesto Maserati and made by the up-and-coming Amadori firm right next door to O.S.C.A. on the *Via Emilia*. A coat of aluminium paint on each wheel conceals a colour which indicates a high percentage of copper in the light alloy. Each spoke is backed up by a radial stiffening rib, giving them a T-section. The wheels are concentrically located by close-fitting raised spigots on the brake drums, and clamped on by five cap screws with relieved heads. This attachment system is adequate for medium-length events with the excellent tyre life now available, but a wheel change would be a double bother as these cap screws appear to require additional tightening to ensure solid mounting after the brake drums have been warmed up. Perhaps this would not be so critical if the cap screws were relieved of braking and drive torques. Wheels and tyres are 15-in., the front rim and tyre sizes being 3.5 and 5.00 respectively, with 4 and 5.25 in use at the rear.

Still built by Morelli in Ferrara, the body is a considerable departure from past O.S.C.A. patterns in both shape and construction. In the former respect it blends a Lister-like nose and lumpy bonnet with a high, full windscreen and a squared, sharply-carved tail that partially encloses the rear wheels. Regarding the latter it features a nose and tail that hinge up and away from the centre of the car to expose chassis and drive components beautifully. Leather straps retain these covers, which have more of an impression of flimsiness than is usual with the tube-framed Morelli body construction.

Seen overall this is truly an O.S.C.A. "special", assembled from a variety of new and old ideas around the shop for the particular benefit of de Tomaso. It envelops their classic Italian chassis with an admittedly Britannic body shell and powers it with a potentially devastating 1,100 c.c. engine. It's new to O.S.C.A. and will take some sorting out, but if that can be accomplished within reasonable time it'll be very, very hard to catch. Even better it may point a new line of endeavour for the patient brothers Maserati. ★

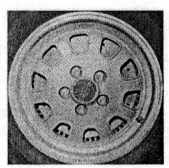

Copper-aluminium alloy wheels made by Amadori have deep T-section spokes for rigidity. Valve stem is metal, retained by nut to avoid shearing off

Osca
Racing Record

Date	Event	Drivers	Car	Position
1953				
8 March	Sebring 12hr	Briggs Cunningham/ Bill Lloyd	Osca MT4	5th place
		Completed 153 laps in Sports 1500 Group Car ran as number 59		
8 March	Sebring 12hr	Rees T. Makins/ Frank Bott	Osca MT4	Not classified
		Completed 115 laps in Sports 1500 Group Car ran as number 6		
25 – 26 April	Mille Miglia	Bruno Venezian/ Achille Albarelli	Osca MT4	12th place
		Car ran as number 340 in the Sports Group		
25 – 26 April	Mille Miglia	Gaetano Sani/ Adone Biachi	Osca MT4	17th place
		Car ran as number 337 in the Sports Group		
25 – 26 April	Mille Miglia	Giuseppe Caoriasco/ L. Gamerro	Osca MT4	26th place
		Car ran as number 358 in the Sports Group		
25 – 26 April	Mille Miglia	Francesco Giardini/ Arrigo Castelli	Osca MT4	93rd place
		Car ran as number 352 in the Sports Group		
25 – 26 April	Mille Miglia	Umberto Bini/ Carlo Lucini	Osca MT4	Did not finish
		Car ran as number 400 in the Sports Group		
25 – 26 April	Mille Miglia	Roberto Sgorbati/ Luigi Zanelli	Osca MT4	Did not finish
		Car ran as number 401 in the Sports Group		
25 – 26 April	Mille Miglia	Giuseppe Pagani/ Walter Forlai	Osca MT4	Did not finish
		Car ran as number 402 in the Sports Group		
25 – 26 April	Mille Miglia	Gianni Balzarini/ Veglia	Osac MT4	Did not finish
		Car ran as number 403 in the Sports Group		
13 – 14 June	Le Mans 24hr	Mario Damonte/ Pierre Louis Dreyfus	Osca MT4	18th place
		Car ran as number 48 completing 232 laps		

Osca
Racing Record

Date	Event	Drivers	Car	Position
13 – 14 June	Le Mans 24hr	Rees T. Makins/ Phil Hill/ Fred Wacker	Osca MT4	Did not finish
		Car ran as number 47 and completed 80 laps		
30 August	Nürburgring 1000km	Nino G. Sani/ Piero Carini	Osca MT4	7th place
		Car ran as number 33 and completed 42 laps		
30 August	Nürburgring 1000km	Armando Francois/ Erwin Bauer	Osca MT4	8th place
		Car ran as number 34 and completed 41 laps		
30 August	Nürburgring 1000km	Francesco Giardini/ Heinrich Sauter	Osca MT4	Did not finish
		Car ran as number 35 in the Sports Group		

1954

Date	Event	Drivers	Car	Position
24 January	Buenos Aires 1000km	Michel Collange/ David Speroni	Osca MT4	11th place
		Car ran as number 74 and completed 85 laps		
24 January	Buenos Aires 1000km	Bob Said/ George Moffett	Osca MT4	Did not finish
7 March	Sebring 12hr	Bill Lloyd/ Stirling Moss	Osca MT4	1st place
		Car ran as number 56 and completed 168 laps		
7 March	Sebring 12hr	James Simpson/ George Colby	Osca MT4	4th place
		Car ran as number 91 and completed 163 laps		
7 March	Sebring 12hr	Otto Linton/ Harry R. Beck	Osca MT4	5th place
		Car ran as number 61 and completed 161 laps		
7 March	Sebring 12hr	Rees T. Makins/ Frank Bott	Osca MT4	8th place
		Car ran as number 65 and completed 152 laps		
7 March	Sebring 12hr	George Moffett/ Bob Said	Osca MT4	Not classified
		Car ran as number 57 and completed 102 laps		
7 March	Sebring 12hr	William Brewster/ Henry Rudkin	Osca MT4	Did not finish
		Car ran as number 58 and completed 47 laps		

Osca
Racing Record

Date	Event	Drivers	Car	Position
1 – 2 May	Mille Miglia	Giulio Cabianca	Osca MT4	10th place
		Car ran as number 343 in the Sports Group		
1 – 2 May	Mille Miglia	Luigi Piotti/ Bruno Cavallari	Osca 2000S	20th place
		Car ran as number 524 in the Sports Group		
13 – 14 June	Le Mans 24hr	Lance Macklin/ Pierre Leygonie/ James Simpson	Osca MT4	Not running at finish
		Car ran as number 43 and completed 254 laps		
13 – 14 June	Le Mans 24hr	Jacques Peron/ Francesco Giardini	Osca MT4	Not running at finish
		Car ran as number 42 and completed 243 laps		
13 – 14 June	Le Mans 24hr	Lucien Farnaud/ Adolfo Macchieraldo	Osca MT4	Did not finish
		Car ran as number 63 and completed 199 laps		
11 September	Tourist Trophy	Ian Burgess/ T. Palmer-Morewood	Osca MT4	Did not finish
		Car ran as number 45 and completed 65 laps		
11 September	Tourist Trophy	Peter B. Reece/ Jackie G. Reece	Osca MT4	Did not finish
		Car ran as number 49 and completed 52 laps		
11 September	Tourist Trophy	Giuseppe Sgorbati/ Lance Macklin	Osca MT4	Did not finish
		Car ran as number 21 and completed 19 laps		
19 – 23 November	Carrera Panamericana	Louis Chiron/ Robert Delpach	Osca MT4	8th place
		Car ran as number 54 in Sports 1500 Group		
19 – 23 November	Carrera Panamericana	Roberto Mieres	Osca MT4	Did not finish
		Car ran as number 52 in Sports 1500 Group		
19 – 23 November	Carrera Panamericana	Manfredo Lippmann	Osca MT4	Did not finish
		Car ran as number 62 in the Sports 1500 Group		

1955

Date	Event	Drivers	Car	Position
13 March	Sebring 12hr	Bill Lloyd/ George Huntoon	Osca MT4	7th place
		Car ran as number 64 and completed 168 laps		

Osca
Racing Record

Date	Event	Drivers	Car	Position
13 March	Sebring 12hr	Carlos Braniff/ Javier Velasquez	Osca MT4	9th place
		Car ran as number 63 and completed 166 laps		
13 March	Sebring 12hr	Otto Linton/ Hal Stetson	Osca MT4	Did not finish
		Car ran as number 73 and completed 83 laps		
13 March	Sebring 12hr	Walt Hansgen/ William Eager	Osca MT4	Did not finish
		Car ran as number 74 and completed 58 laps		
13 March	Sebring 12hr	Phil Stewart/ Ted Boynton	Osca MT4	Did not finish
		Car ran as number 66 and completed 33 laps		
13 March	Sebring 12hr	Harry A. Chapman	Osca MT4	Did not finish
		Car ran as number 65 and completed 18 laps		
30 April – 1 May	Mille Miglia	Luc Descollanges/ Robert Nicol	Osca MT4	14th place
		Car ran as number 542 in the Sports Group		
30 April – 1 May	Mille Miglia	Claude Bourillot	Osca MT4	24th place
		Car ran as number 518 in the Sports Group		
30 April – 1 May	Mille Miglia	Raffaele Foglia/ Arnaldo Colantoni	Osca MT4	33rd place
		Car ran as number 533 in the Sports Group		
30 April – 1 May	Mille Miglia	Luigi Nobile/ Luigi Bettiol	Osca MT4	34th place
		Car ran as number 532 in the Sports Group		
30 April – 1 May	Mille Miglia	Carlo Monzino/ R.G. d'Artogna	Osca MT4	73rd place
		Car ran as number 526 in the Sports Group		
30 April – 1 May	Mille Miglia	Bruno Franzoni/ Bruno Gavazzoli	Osca MT4	80th place
		Car ran as number 525 in the Sports Group		
30 April – 1 May	Mille Miglia	Giulio Cabianco	Osca MT4	Did not finish
		Car ran as number 546 in the Sports Group		
30 April – 1 May	Mille Miglia	Bruno Ricciardi/ Angelo Sbordone	Osca MT4	Did not finish
		Car ran as number 512 in the Sports Group		
30 April – 1 May	Mille Miglia	Carlo Falli	Osca MT4	Did not finish
		Car ran as number 515 in the Sports Group		

Osca
Racing Record

Date	Event	Drivers	Car	Position
30 April – 1 May	Mille Miglia	Roberto Sgorbati	Osca MT4	Did not finish
		Car ran as number 558 in the Sports Group		
11 – 12 June	Le Mans 24hr	Giulio Cabianca/ Giuseppe Scorbatti	Osca MT4	11th place
		Car ran as number 40 and completed 256 laps		
16 October	Targa Florio	Giulio Cabianca/ Piero Carini	Osca MT4	7th place
		Car ran as number 64 and completed 13 laps		
16 October	Targa Florio	Domenico Rotolo/ Luigi de Pasquale	Osca MT4	14th place
		Car ran as number 42 and completed 12 laps		
16 October	Targa Florio	Bruno Ricciari/ Angelo Sbordone	Osca MT4	Did not finish
		Car ran as number 54 and completed 6 laps		

1956

Date	Event	Drivers	Car	Position
28 – 29 April	Mille Miglia	Giulio Cabianca	Osca MT4	9th place
		Car ran as number 428 in the Sports Group		
28 – 29 April	Mille Miglia	Attilio Brandi	Osca MT4	62nd place
		Car ran as number 404 in the Sports Group		
28 – 29 April	Mille Miglia	Ovidio Capelli	Osca S750	106th place
		Car ran as number 210 in the Sports Group		
28 – 29 April	Mille Miglia	Carlo Falli	Osca MT4	125th place
		Car ran as number 406 in the Sports Group		
28 – 29 April	Mille Miglia	Umberto Maglioli	Osca MT4	Did not finish
		Car ran as number 428 in the Sports Group		
28 – 29 April	Mille Miglia	Luigi Villoresi	Osca MT4	Did not finish
		Car ran as number 436 in the Sports Group		
28 – 29 April	Mille Miglia	Luois Chiron	Osca S750	Did not finish
		Car ran as number 215 in the Sports Group		
28 – 29 April	Mille Miglia	Nando Cattani	Osca MT4	Did not finish
		Car ran as number 358 in the Sports Group		
28 – 29 April	Mille Miglia	Umberto Bini	Osca MT4	Did not finish
		Car ran as number 402 in the Sports Group		
28 – 29 April	Mille Miglia	Rinaldo Masperi/ Erasmo Foglietti	Osca MT4	Did not finish
		Car ran as number 409 in the Sports Group		

Osca
Racing Record

Date	Event	Drivers	Car	Position
28 – 29 July	Le Mans 24hr	Jean Laroche/ Remy Radix	Osca S750	Did not finish

Car ran as number 42 and completed 4 laps

1957

Date	Event	Drivers	Car	Position
20 January	Buenos Aires 1000km	Alejandro De Tomaso/ Isabel Haskell	Osca MT4	6th place

Car ran as number 62 and completed 88 laps

20 January	Buenos Aires 1000km	Sergio Vivaldi/ Lino Fayen	Osca MT4	Not running at finish

Car ran as number 64 and completed 71 laps

20 January	Buenos Aires 1000km	Enrique Arrieta/ Carlos Guimarey	Osca MT4	Did not finish

Car ran as number 58 and completed 14 laps

23 March	Sebring 12hr	Harry R. Beck/ Hal Stetson/ Otto Linton	Osca MT4	13th place

Car ran as number 47 and completed 170 laps

23 March	Sebring 12hr	Alejandro De Tomaso/ Isabel Haskell	Osca MT4	Did not finish

Car ran as number 67 and completed 70 laps

11 – 12 May	Mille Miglia	Giulio Cabianca	Osca S950	26th place

Car ran as number 325 in the Sports Group

11 – 12 May	Mille Miglia	Corrado Manfredini	Osca MT4	53rd place

Car ran as number 329 in the Sports Group

11 – 12 May	Mille Miglia	Giancarlo Rigamonte	Osca S750	58th place

Car ran as number 138 in the Sports Group

11 – 12 May	Mille Miglia	Jean Laroche/ Remy Radix	Osca S750	61st place

Car ran as number 151 in the Sports Group

11 – 12 May	Mille Miglia	Carlo Falli	Osca MT4	62nd place

Car ran as number 326 in the Sports Group

11 – 12 May	Mille Miglia	Gustavo Laureati	Osca S750	72nd place

Car ran as number 159 in the Sports Group

11 – 12 May	Mille Miglia	Rinaldo Masperi/ Erasmo Foglietti	Osca MT4	143rd place

Car ran as number 332 in the Sports Group

Osca
Racing Record

Date	Event	Drivers	Car	Position
11 – 12 May	Mille Miglia	Giuseppe Maugeri/ Antonio Barbagallo	Osca MT4	152nd place
		Car ran as number 334 in the Sports Group		
11 – 12 May	Mille Miglia	Piero Bernabei	Osca MT4	Did not finish
		Car ran as number 330 in the Sports Group		
11 – 12 May	Mille Miglia	Lamberto Gerosi	Osca MT4	Did not finish
		Car ran as number 335 in the Sports Group		
11 – 12 May	Mille Miglia	Attilo Brandi/ Vannini	Osca MT4	Did not finish
		Car ran as number 340 in the Sports Group		
11 – 12 May	Mille Miglia	Vladimiro Toselli	Osca 1500S	Did not finish
		Car ran as number 332 in the Sports Group		
22 – 23 June	Le Mans 24hr	Jean Laroche/ Remy Radix	Osca S750	19th place
		Car ran as number 46 and completed 234 laps		
11 August	Swedish G.P.	Jon Fast/ Gunnar Bengston	Osca 1500TN	16th place
		Car ran as number 34 and completed 120 laps		
11 August	Swedish G.P.	Alejandro De Tomaso/ Isabel Haskell	Osca 1500TN	Did not finish
		Car ran as number 31 and completed 30 laps		
3 November	Venezuelan G.P.	Umberto Masetti/ Andre Testut	Osca MT4	11th place
		Car ran as number 76 and completed 86 laps		
3 November	Venezuelan G.P.	Alejandro De Tomaso/ Isabel Haskell	Osca MT4	Did not finish
		Car ran as number 62 and completed 14 laps		

1958

Date	Event	Drivers	Car	Position
26 January	Buenos Aires 1000km	Roberto Bonomi/ Luigi Piotti	Osca MT4	Not running at finish
		Car ran as number 42 and completed 75 laps		
26 January	Buenos Aires 1000km	A. Rodriguez-Laretta/ M. de Filippis	Osca MT4	Did not finish
		Car ran as number 40 and completed 71 laps		

Osca
Racing Record

Date	Event	Drivers	Car	Position
26 January	Buenos Aires 1000km	Alejandro De Tomaso/ Isabel Haskell	Osca MT4	Did not finish
		Car ran as number 46 and completed 5 laps		
22 March	Sebring 12hr	Alejandro De Tomaso/ Isabel Haskell	Osca S750	8th place
		Car ran as number 60 and completed 175 laps		
22 March	Sebring 12hr	Hal Stetson/ Otto Linton	Osca MT4	13th place
		Car ran as number 47 and completed 170 laps		
11 May	Targa Florio	Giulio Cabianca/ Franco Bordoni	Osca MT4	5th place
		Car ran as number 72 and completed 14 laps		
11 May	Targa Florio	Guido Garufi/ Lorenzo Melarosa	Osca MT4	Did not finish
		Car ran as number 54 in the Sports Group		
11 May	Targa Florio	Giuseppe Rossi/ Enzo Buzzetti	Osca 1100S	Did not finish
		Car ran as number 64 in the Sports Group		
11 May	Targa Florio	Domenico Rotolo/ Luigi Di Pasquale	Osca 1100S	Did not finish
		Car ran as number 66 in the Sports Group		
11 May	Targa Florio	Luciana Mantovani/ Ludovico Scarfiotti	Osca MT4	Did not finish
		Car ran as number 74 in the Sports Group		
11 May	Targa Florio	Colin Davis	Osca MT4	Did not finish
		Car ran as number 70 in the Sports Group		
1 June	Nürburgring 1000km	Jon Fast/ J. Campbell-Jones	Osca MT4	11th place
		Car ran as number 25 and completed 42 laps		
1 June	Nürburgring 1000km	Gordon Fowell/ Derek Godfrey	Osca MT4	Did not finish
		Car ran as number 26 and completed 16 laps		
21 – 22 June	Le Mans 24hr	Alejandro De Tomaso/ Colin Davis	Osca S750TN	11th place
		Car ran as number 42 and completed 252 laps		

Osca
Racing Record

Date	Event	Drivers	Car	Position
21 – 22 June	Le Mans 24hr	Jean Laroche/ Remy Radix	Osca S750	14th place

Car ran as number 60 and completed 241 laps

1959

Date	Event	Drivers	Car	Position
21 March	Sebring 12hr	Alejandro De Tomaso/ Denise McCluggage	Osca S750	18th place

Car ran as number 60 and completed 161 laps

Date	Event	Drivers	Car	Position
21 March	Sebring 12hr	Carl Haas/ Frank Campbell	Osca 1500S	Did not finish

Car ran as number 38 and completed 115 laps

Date	Event	Drivers	Car	Position
21 March	Sebring 12hr	Ricardo Rodriguez/ Frank Bott	Osca S950	Did not finish

Car ran as number 56 and completed 106 laps

Date	Event	Drivers	Car	Position
21 March	Sebring 12hr	A. Markelson/ Rees T. Makins	Osca S750	Did not finish

Car ran as number 61 and completed 82 laps

Date	Event	Drivers	Car	Position
24 May	Targa Florio	Umberto Bini/ Luciano Mantovani	Osca 1100S [1184]	7th place

Car ran as number 84 and completed 14 laps

Date	Event	Drivers	Car	Position
24 May	Targa Florio	Domenico Rotolo/ Gaspare Cavaliere	Osca 1100S	11th place

Car ran as number 72 and completed 14 laps

Date	Event	Drivers	Car	Position
24 May	Targa Florio	Sesto Leonardi/ Alfredo Tinazzo	Osca S750	17th place

Car ran as number 50 and completed 14 laps

Date	Event	Drivers	Car	Position
24 May	Targa Florio	Gustavo Laureati/ Giuseppe Celani	Osca S750	19th place

Car ran as number 60 and completed 14 laps

Date	Event	Drivers	Car	Position
24 May	Targa Florio	Giancarlo Rigamonti/ Anna Maria Peduzzi	Osca S750	20th place

Car ran as number 56 and completed 14 laps

Date	Event	Drivers	Car	Position
24 May	Targa Florio	Francesco la Mattina/ Armando Soldano	Osca 1100S	Did not finish

Car ran as number 74 in the Sports Group

Osca
Racing Record

Date	Event	Drivers	Car	Position
24 May	Targa Florio	Emauele Trapani/ Bartolomeo Donata	Osca 1100S	Did not finish
		Car ran as number 78 in the Sports Group		
24 May	Targa Florio	Enzo Buzzetti/ Giuseppe Rossi	Osca 1100S	Did not finish
		Car ran as number 82 in the Sports Group		
24 May	Targa Florio	Eduardo Lualdi-Gabardi/ Ludovico Scarfiotti	Osca MT4	Did not finish
		Car ran as number 14 in the Sports Group		
7 June	Nürburgring 1000km	Colin Davis/ Alejandro De Tomaso	Osca 1500S	Did not finish
		Car ran as number 30 in the Sports Group		
7 June	Nürburgring 1000km	Isabel Haskell/ Denise McCluggage	Osca 1500S	Did not finish
		Car ran as number 31 in the Sports Group		
20 – 21 June	Le Mans 24hr	Jean Laroche/ Andre Testut	Osca S750	Did not finish
		Car ran as number 52 and completed 88 laps		
20 – 21 June	Le Mans 24hr	Pedro Rodriguez/ Ricardo Rodriguez	Osca S750TN	Did not finish
		Car ran as number 51 and completed 32 laps		

1960

Date	Event	Drivers	Car	Position
26 March	Sebring 12hr	John Bentley/ John Gordon	Osca S750	12th place
		Car ran as number 63 and completed 170 laps		
26 March	Sebring 12hr	George Koehne/ Rees T. Makins	Osca MT4	13th place
		Car ran as number 47 and completed 169 laps		
26 March	Sebring 12hr	David Cunningham/ John Fulp	Osca S750	23rd place
		Car ran as number 65 and completed 162 laps		
26 March	Sebring 12hr	Denise McCluggage/ Marianne Rollo	Osca S750	Did not finish
		Car ran as number 64 and completed 34 laps		

Osca
Racing Record

Date	Event	Drivers	Car	Position
8 May	Targa Florio	Ada Pace/ Giancarlo Castellina	Osca 1100S	11th place
		Car ran as number 74 and completed 10 laps		
8 May	Targa Florio	Gianni Brichetti/ Carrado Manfredini	Osca 1500S	15th place
		Car ran as number 156 and completed 10 laps		
8 May	Targa Florio	Francesco Siracuso/ A.M. Peduzzi	Osca 1500S	17th place
		Car ran as number 152 and completed 10 laps		
8 May	Targa Florio	Attilio Brandi/ Ilfo Minzoni	Osca 1100S	24th place
		Car ran as number 84 and completed 10 laps		
8 May	Targa Florio	Domenico Rotolo/ Gaspare Cavaliere	Osca MT4	Not running at finish
		Car ran as number 82 and completed 7 laps		
8 May	Targa Florio	Giovanni Giordano/ Gaetano Starrabba	Osca MT4	Did not finish
		Car ran as number 154 in the Sports Group		
8 May	Targa Florio	Mario Raimondo Salvatore Calascibetta	Osca MT4	Did not finish
		Car ran as number 76 and completed 7 laps		
8 May	Targa Florio	Umberto Bini	Osca 1100S	Did not finish
		Car ran as number 80 in the Sports Group		
8 May	Targa Florio	George Bauer	Osca 1500S	Did not finish
		Car ran as number 162 in the Sports Group		
25 – 26 June	Le Mans 24hr	John Bentley/ John Gordon	Osca S750	18th place
		Car ran as number 54 and completed 237 laps		
25 – 26 June	Le Mans 24hr	Jean Laroche/ Andre Simon	Osca S750	Did not finish
		Car ran as number 53 and completed 66 laps		

1961

Date	Event	Drivers	Car	Position
25 March	Sebring 12hr	George Peck/ John Hoffman/ Robert Richardson	Osca S750	20th place
		Car ran as number 71 and completed 171 laps		

Osca
Racing Record

Date	Event	Drivers	Car	Position
25 March	Sebring 12hr	David Cunningham/ Den Price	Osca 1000S	Did not finish
		Car ran as number 69 in the Sports Group		
30 April	Targa Florio	Umberto Bini/ Giancarlo Rigamonti	Osca 1000S	15th place
		Car ran as number 70 and completed 10 laps		
30 April	Targa Florio	Ludovico Scarfiotti/ Colin Davis	Osca 1500S	Not running at finish
		Car ran as number 120 and completed 9 laps		
30 April	Targa Florio	Gregorio Filippone/ Francesco Patane	Osca MT4	Not running at finish
		Car ran as number 74 and completed 7 laps		
30 April	Targa Florio	Mario Raimondo/ C. D'Angelo	Osca 1000S	Did not finish
		Car ran as number 72 and completed 6 laps		
30 April	Targa Florio	M. de Luca di Lizzano/ Attilio Brandi	Osca 1000S	Did not finish
		Car ran as number 60 and completed 6 laps		
30 April	Targa Florio	Domenico Rotolo/ Salvatore Sirchia	Osca MT4	Did not finish
		Car ran as number 64 and completed 5 laps		
10 – 11 June	Le Mans 24hr	David Cunningham/ Ed Hugus	Osca 1100S	Did not finish
		Car ran as number 43 and completed 125 laps		
10 – 11 June	Le Mans 24hr	Jean Laroche/ Colin Davis	Osca S750	Did not finish
		Car ran as number 50 and completed 85 laps		
15 August	Pescara 4hr	Colin Davis	Osca 1600S	5th place
		Car ran as number 28 and completed 21 laps		
15 August	Pescara 4hr	Umberto Bini	Osca 1000S	8th place
		Car ran as number 56 and completed 20 laps		
15 August	Pescara 4hr	Leandro Terra	Osca 1600S	13th place
		Car ran as number 30 and completed 20 laps		
15 August	Pescara 4hr	Attilio Brandi/ Adolfo Tedeschi	Osca 1000S	20th place
		Car ran as number 66 and completed 20 laps		

Osca
Racing Record

Date	Event	Drivers	Car	Position
15 August	Pescara 4hr	Gregorio Filippone	Osca MT4	28th place
		Car ran as number 50 and completed 17 laps		
15 August	Pescara 4hr	Sesto Leonardi/ C.A. Del Bue	Osca 1000S	Not classified
		Car ran as number 72 in the Sports Group		
15 August	Pescara 4hr	Ludovico Scarfiotti	Osca 2000S	Did not finish
		Car ran as number 24 and completed 3 laps		

1962

Date	Event	Drivers	Car	Position
24 March	Sebring 12hr	H.S. Lichtie/ Robert Publicker	Osca 1600GT	Did not finish
		Car ran as number 58 and completed 33 laps		
24 March	Sebring 12hr	Denise McCluggage/ Allen Eager	Osca 1000S	Did not finish
		Car ran as number 77 and completed 10 laps		
6 May	Targa Florio	Domenico Rotolo/ Sergio Mantia	Osca MT4	Did not finish
		Car ran as number 110 and completed 5 laps		
6 May	Targa Florio	Ludovico Scarfiotti	Osca 2000S	Did not finish
		Car ran as number 118 and completed 3 laps		
23 – 24 June	Le Mans 24hr	George Arents/ Jose Behra	Osca 1600GT	Did not finish
		Car ran as number 37 and completed 227 laps		
23 – 24 June	Le Mans 24hr	John Bentley/ John Gordon	Osca 1600GT	Did not finish
		Car ran as number 36 and completed 13 laps		
16 September	Bridgehampton Double 400	Denise McCluggage/ Allen Eager	Osca 1000S	Did not finish
		Car ran as number 23 and completed 42 laps		

1963

Date	Event	Drivers	Car	Position
23 March	Sebring 12hr	Thomas T. Fleming/ Harold Baumann	Osca 1600GT	Not classified
		Car ran as number 57 and completed 139 laps		
23 March	Sebring 12hr	Burrel Besancon/ Robert Publicker	Osca 1600GT	Did not finish
		Car ran as number 56 and completed 41 laps		

Osca
Racing Record

Date	Event	Drivers	Car	Position
2 June	Consuma Hillclimb	Gianfranco Stanga	Osca 2000S	7th place
		Car ran as number 4 in the Sports Group		
2 June	Consuma Hillclimb	Sesto Leonardi	Osca 1000S	16th place
		Car ran as number 26 in the Sports Group		
2 June	Consuma Hillclimb	Attilio Brandi	Osca 1000S	32nd place
		Car ran as number 20 in the Sports Group		
2 June	Consuma Hillclimb	Mario Nardari	Osca 1600GT	34th place
		Car ran as number 74 in the Grand Touring Group		
2 June	Consuma Hillclimb	Ottorini Zarattin	Osca 1600GT	67th place
		Car ran as number 72 in the Grand Touring Group		

1964

Date	Event	Drivers	Car	Position
26 April	Targa Florio	Mario Nardani/ Ottorini Zarattin	Osca 1600GT2	27th place
		Car ran as number 56 and completed 8 laps		
26 April	Targa Florio	Domenico Rotolo/ Filippo di Liberto	Osca MT4	Did not finish
		Car ran as number 164 and completed 2 laps		
24 May	Consuma Hillclimb	P.L. Muccini	Osca 1000S	44th place
		Car ran as number 339 in the Sports Group		
24 May	Consuma Hillclimb	Giorgio Tossi	Osca 1000S	112th place
		Car ran as number 341 in the Sports Group		
24 May	Consuma Hillclimb	Ottorini Zarattin	Osca 1600GT2	123rd place
		Car ran as number 319 in the Grand Touring Group		
24 May	Consuma Hillclimb	I. Malandrucco	Osca 1000S	178th place
		Car ran as number 342 in the Sports Group		
24 May	Consuma Hillclimb	Augusto Nardari	Osca 1600GT	Did not finish
		Car ran as number 321 in the Grand Touring Group		

Osca
Racing Record

Date	Event	Drivers	Car	Position
30 August	Swiss Mountain G.P.	Roger Rey	Osca 2000S	31st place

Car ran as number 51 in the Racing Group

1965

6 June	Circuit of Mugello	P.L. Muccini/ F. Boroni	Osca 1000S	19th place

Car ran as number 53 in the Sports-Racing Group

6 June	Circuit of Mugello	Luigi Malanca/ Luigi Foschi	Osca 1500S	26th place

Car ran as number 72 in the Sports-Racing Group

6 June	Circuit of Mugello	Giuseppe Rossi	Osca MT4	29th place

Car ran as number 67 in the Sports-Racing Group

29 August	Swiss Mountain G.P.	Roger Rey	Osca 1500S	40th place

Car ran as number 164 in the Sports-Racing/Prototype Group

1966

17 July	Circuit of Mugello	Giuseppe Rossi	Osca MT4	38th place

Car ran as number 175 in the Prototype Group

28 August	Swiss Mountain G.P.	Erwin Schnewlin	Osca 1100S	30th place

Car ran as number 173 in the Prototype Group

1967

6 August	Enna City Cup	Silvano Scodellari	Osca 1100S	10th place

Car ran as number 6 and completed 50 laps

1970

3 May	Targa Florio	Mario Spataro/ Claudio Bruschi	Osca 1000S	48th place

Car ran as number 252 and completed 7 laps

Moretti
750 Gran Sport

A LESSON IN SMALL THINGS

Words and pictures by Johann Lemercier

Moretti

When it comes to nimble 750cc sports coupes from Italy, the first names that come to mind are usually Abarth and Zagato. Yet it was a rather different association which brought about the car featured here: an exceptional collaboration between Moretti and Michelotti.

Giovanni Moretti was a self-made man with a passion for a job well done, who had begun producing cars in 1948 after many active years spent learning all aspects of the trade – and manufacturing electric trucks. He took great pride in the hand-crafted quality of his products and never actually surrendered to mass-production methods, electing to concentrate on coachbuilding activities in the early 1960s. A close collaboration with Fiat ensued, leading to several attractive 850-based coupe derivatives.

Likewise, Giovanni Michelotti knew a thing or two about designing cars. By 1953, when he penned the lines of this Moretti coupe, he had already put his signature to models built over some of the most prestigious chassis the world's manufacturers could offer. Better known until then for his interpretations of Ferrari, Lancia, Alfa Romeo and Maserati running gear, he was also keen to lend his hand to more marginal projects such as the Cunningham C3. Yet perhaps this diminutive berlinetta was the most significant challenge he had faced until then, for shaping the proportions on a car of such minuscule dimensions and turning it into an object of elegance is a significantly harder task than working on a larger chassis.

The young Torinese stylist pulled out all the stops to make the design work from every angle, using every visual trick known to him and inventing quite a few more. While nowadays designers rely on gigantic wheels to make their creations more dramatic, Michelotti went the opposite way, cleverly making use of the car's restrained dimensions to make the wheels appear bigger. He opened clean wheel-arches with discreet flares, balanced against a low slab-side profile and smallish side-windows for maximum effect. On the top surfaces, the colour division which at that time still identified most of his styling efforts played a great part in lightening the overall volume of the body.

The extra-short front overhang was made possible by the position of the small engine, set way back in the chassis, which Moretti's designers had created with racing in mind. The longer rear overhang reveals another visual trick: the tail is actually pointy. The extended centreline profile expresses dynamic motion as the eye picks up the extra muscle over the rear wheels, yet the rear corners of the car quickly wrap behind the wheels and instill a sense of compact determination. Stability, stance, stamina: the Gran Sport's body had it all.

Difficult though it may be to assess the car's size from looking at it in photographs, the steering wheel gives the game away: seen from the tail, it appears to fill half the cabin! Despite this, the interior does not feel as Spartan as one would suspect. Not only is it neatly trimmed, but the very low seating position actually makes sense. A fair amount of headroom and generous daylight openings positively alleviate any risk of claustrophobia, while the far-back positioning of the seats provides ample leg room. The seats themselves only offer minimal cushioning and typically short wraparound backrests. There is no boot-lid and the Plexiglas rear window is fixed (no tailgates in those days), which leaves space in the rear of the cabin which ends where the body does, with plenty of room for a moderately accessible spare wheel. Not the best car over long distances, perhaps? Ponder this: Moretti 750s were involved in publicity stunts such as the 17,000km Algiers-Cape Town or the 'All Continents Rally' (Rallye di tutti i Continenti), which ended in 1955 after 120,000km had been covered.

The rectangular-section tubular chassis is roughly based on a backbone design, the main chassis frame members concentrated around the engine, gearbox and driveshaft forming a stiff central tunnel area. Needless to say, the body is all aluminium, and non-stressed structures – such as the bonnet frame – are drilled to save weight. Potent drum brakes all round (aluminium at the front) make stopping an easy task. The only grievances lie with the somewhat vague steering and a tendency for the car to understeer, yet the fairly straightforward suspension layout gets the job done efficiently. Two pairs of parallel quarter-elliptic springs are combined at the front with tubular dampers, whereas similar leaf springs act as trailing arms to guide the rear live axle. As a result, the ride is firm but not brutal and confirms the Gran Sport's relevance both on and off the track. Brisk acceleration is delivered through a four-speed gearbox, of which the top three gears are synchronised.

The 748cc twin cam engine is a sprightly little warrior. Mounted in the engine bay is a five-main-bearing competition unit (built in a limited number in 1955) in place of the normal   ↪

51

Moretti

Moretti 750 Gran Sport

production three-main-bearing motor, which could not be reunited with the car despite incessant efforts from successive owners to acquire it. Another departure from the original configuration is the use of two sidedraught instead of downdraught Weber carburettors.

The twin chain-driven overhead camshafts assist in developing a power output in the region of 70bhp at a healthy 7000rpm. This figure becomes attractive when one realises that the car only weighed 495kg. The exhaust line is pretty much a straight tube all the way with just a tiny muffler, delivering a crisp engine note which is more motorcycle than car. *Road & Track* tested a similar berlinetta back in 1954 and raved about it: their reliable measurements revealed a top speed near the 100mph mark. In essence, though, its performance can only be deemed modest nowadays, when at the time the Moretti 750 was pure race-bred machinery. The absence of bumpers, the prominent fuel-filler cap on the rear deck and the rugged but smart steel wheels all provide clues to its true temperament.

Production figures for the coupe remain a mystery. Few have made it to the present day and, though they were produced for four years (1953-1957), this Gran Sport berlinetta is surely a very rare item. The lack of reliable records also prevents us from establishing the early history of this particular example, but intriguingly it was one of quite a number of Morettis imported to the US (half a dozen cars may not sound like much but it could have accounted for nearly half the total run). In spite of the noted American aversion to such diminutive motoring, Morettis earned a good reputation on the track Stateside.

Well-known car historian Karl Ludvigsen unearthed it in 1979, and after years in oblivion the Moretti was subject to a

ABOVE LEFT: During the 1950s Moretti built its own engines. This twin cam unit develops 70bhp at 7000rpm. The car weighs just 495kg

full restoration. The unique egg-crate grille which differentiates it from its sister cars was crafted in California during the 1950s by hot-rod artist Von Dutch, and it was decided to maintain it in the course of a new and very thorough rejuvenation completed in April this year. Not only was it considered to be now part of the car's inherent history, but it also fits it perfectly – which cannot hurt. At the time of printing the car was only missing the dashboard-mounted rear-view mirror (making it a bit of a hazard in traffic) and the original hubcaps. Truth is, the wheels look better without!

The Gran Sport was on its way to America literally minutes after we took our photographs. There it will join the ranks of the Lawrence Auriana Collection in Connecticut, one of the (if not the) most impressive collections of Italian sports and racing cars in the world. Its addition to the line-up really fills a significant gap and underlines Moretti's rightful place in automotive history.

Carrozzeria Moretti has long been overlooked by historians and collectors alike. In the early 1950s Moretti was a manufacturer in his own right, and his story is a key to understanding the Italian motoring backdrop of the time. Too often dismissed as an artisan merely crafting Fiat specials in his backyard, Giovanni Moretti was in fact a consummate entrepreneur animated by a strong drive to excel in all areas of workmanship and there is, in fact, nothing borrowed from Fiat in our featured car. Here was a man who knew where he stood and was happy to remain a small-scale manufacturer as long as the quality of his products was unquestioned. Clients agreed to pay a consistent premium for that devotion to excellence and those few devotees kept him in business until other manufacturers were able to mass-produce models of similar displacement at a fraction of the cost.

● *Special thanks to Dott Adolfo Orsi and Historica Selecta, who coordinated the restoration of the car with Modena-based specialists.*

Moretti

TECHNICAL SPECIFICATIONS	
Manufacture:	1953-1957
Engine:	748cc in-line 4, DOHC
Bore & stroke:	60mm x 66mm
Compression ratio:	10.0:1
Fuel feed:	2 side-draft double-barrel Weber 42DCO3s
Power:	71bhp @ 7000rpm
Torque:	n/a
Power to weight ratio:	143bhp/tonne
Transmission:	Moretti 4-speed manual, rwd
Body:	All aluminium
Brakes:	Finned aluminium drums front; steel drums rear
Suspension:	Twin 1/4-elliptic springs & dampers front; live axle with twin 1/4-elliptic springs as trailing arms & dampers rear
Wheels:	15in
Tyres:	Michelin135SR15 (originally Pirelli, 4.25 section)
Dimensions:	3290mm (L), 1372mm (W), 1168mm (H), 1963mm (wheelbase), 1220mm (fr track), 1156mm (rear track)
Kerb weight:	1090lb (495kg)
0-60mph:	15.5sec
Top speed:	100mph
Cost when new:	$(US)3,500.00

Moretti

Moretti 2300S Cabriolet

Moretti

PURPOSE-BUILT TOWN CARS AND REBODIED FIATS

Moretti first built their own complete small cars, but began to concentrate on rebodied Fiats when things became difficult

THE MORETTI COMPANY is by no means one of the most famous car manufacturers to come from that ultra-productive area of Northern Italy around Turin and Milan. Indeed, with neighbours like Ferrari, Lamborghini, Maserati, Fiat, Alfa Romeo and Lancia, mostly marques that are surrounded by a mystical aura of speed and comfort combined with that unique stamp of Italian styling, the Moretti would have to be something very special to be realistic competition. Instead of attempting to compete with the luxury makers, Fabbrica Automobili Moretti SpA of Turin took the only other course available to them in the early 1960s: their maxim was: 'If you can't beat them, give up and start looking for a new area in which to sell'.

The little company, that had once taken great pains to build complete cars with 'home-made' engines, decided to divert into the manufacture of variations on the models of a larger marque, Fiat. In this field they had a better chance of survival for it would be cheaper for one man to indulge in his own designs of car body than to spend a large amount of money developing complete cars that had just a small chance of nibbling

Right: the first car produced by Giovanni Moretti, and separate from the actual Moretti company, was this two-seater, rear-engined convertible which he built in 1927

Below: the Moretti La Cita was built from 1945 until 1948. It was powered by a twin-cylinder 350 cc engine which developed 14 bhp and gave the car a top speed of 85 kph

Moretti

at the cake of the then-thriving car-buying market. What better way to go about this than to shelter under the wing of Fiat, one of Europe's industrial giants, who would supply rolling chassis, complete with engines.

Moretti's own original cars were essentially of the mini type; the first, built in 1946, was called La Cita. This was powered by a front-mounted, 14 bhp, vertical-twin engine of 350 cc, which was obviously very economical. Based on a tubular frame, the car also featured hydraulic brakes and independent front suspension. The La Cita was originally available only as a saloon, but estate and coupé versions were later added to the catalogues, the latter having a claimed top speed of 60 mph and the ability to cover up to eighty miles on one gallon of petrol. Developed alongside the ohv twin-cylinder power unit was a four-cylinder

Above: towards the end of the 1960s, Moretti produced this neat 850 cc coupé. It used a rear-mounted Fiat engine driving the rear wheels

Below: Moretti's 750 coupé built during the early 1950s

twin-overhead-camshaft engine, which was later to be used in a Formula Three chassis. By 1950, the 350 cc La Cita was available in 600 and 750 cc forms, based on backbone chassis as opposed to the space-frame design used previously.

Still on the small-car theme, 27 bhp two-bearing single-cam and 51 bhp three-bearing twin-cam derivatives of the saloon's vertical twin were in production in that car by 1954. Moretti's Turin neighbours, Michelotti, did a styling exercise on a 1.2-litre Moretti chassis which was to retail in America at the high price of 2900 dollars. After experiments with that peculiarly Italian device, the small-engined commercial, as well as four-door versions of the saloon, the step was taken to build a new car based on the Fiat 500 Nuova; this was in 1957.

Moretti

Although this transition to rebodied production cars had taken place, for a time, a large range of Moretti's own cars could still be purchased. They were as follows: in 750 cc form, there were two single-cam saloons, the 27 bhp and the 43 bhp, designated Super, there was a buzzy little twin-cam GT, an 820 cc estate, a 1-litre 50 bhp saloon and, by now, the Formula Junior rear-engined racer. The racer was built and driven by Aquilino Branca, who was later to build Formula Three cars under his own name, and had moderate if not outstanding success. Branca did not actually work with Moretti, but had an agreement that he would be able to use the company's advertising and marketing as long as Branca's cars, which were some of the first to feature mid-mounted engines, carried Moretti's badge. On the production front, there was also a neat little coupé called the Golden Arrow. It featured Dunlop disc brakes and, like all the other

Above: in 1962, Moretti marketed this attractive convertible named the 2500SS. It used the six-cylinder Fiat engine

Below: a 1963 Moretti 1500 coupé. Like most Morettis, it used Fiat engine parts

production cars, coil and wishbone suspension. As can be seen, the range was very large for a small company, but unfortunately only a hundred or so cars were actually sold in 1958, obviously nowhere near enough to warrant such a large selection which composed, primarily, mini cars for the ever-growing small-car market.

The company's name was changed to Moretti Fabbrica Automobili e Stabilimenti Carrozzeria SAS in 1962, this coinciding with the decision to concentrate on rebodied Fiats. A large step up market was taken with a convertible based on Fiat's six-cylinder 2300, the engine of which was enlarged to 2.5 litres to produce a very respectable 163 bhp. This stayed in production for but a year, from 1962 to '63.

Thereafter, with Moretti's own cars gone, the company built a range of cars on the Fiat 500 and 850 chassis. A large range of engines was available in both

Moretti

saloon, coupé and estate-car bodies. These were of 500, 595 and 850 cc sizes. By 1970, Moretti had been taken under the Fiat umbrella, selling their cars through the organisation's large network. One of the most popular vehicles on the market at this time was the Midimaxi, a Citroën Mehari-type 'Jeep', based on Fiat 127 front-wheel-drive mechanical parts. Other cars to be seen were De-luxe and Sport versions of many popular Fiats, looking not too different, but just enough so for them to find a ready market. One interesting exercise was a 132 safety coupé which featured faired-in headlamps and rubber strips around the car's perimeter.

In 1977 there were about eighty employees at Moretti's factory, in via Monginevro, Turin, producing cars of similar concept to the rival Giannini and concentrating on a revised Maxi model based on the 1977 Fiat 127 and on a Fiat 126 based design.

Moretti's raison d'être has been to bring a degree of style and snob-appeal to the mass-production car market, to offer subtle one-upmanship in the eyes of Moretti owners and to profit from doing so. Moretti's business is on a modest scale, its aspirations are exotic and its products perhaps are overpriced. Only the uncertainty of the Italian economy casts doubt on the company's future: exclusivity always has been, and always will be, a sought after commodity.   LJC

Right: built by Moretti and sold through the Fiat organisation's network was the Midimaxi of 1970. It used a Fiat 127 engine driving the front wheels

Below: an attractive example of Moretti's work on Fiat chassis is this 1976 car based on the 128 3P Coupé. Although a little heavier than the standard car, the better aerodynamics of the Moretti mean that performance is unaltered

58

Moretti

Moretti 1500 Cabriolet

Moretti 1500 Coupe

Moretti

Moretti 2300S Coupe

Moretti

Moretti Coupe 2 + 2 Dragster (rear)

Moretti Coupe 2 + 2 Dragster (front)

Moretti

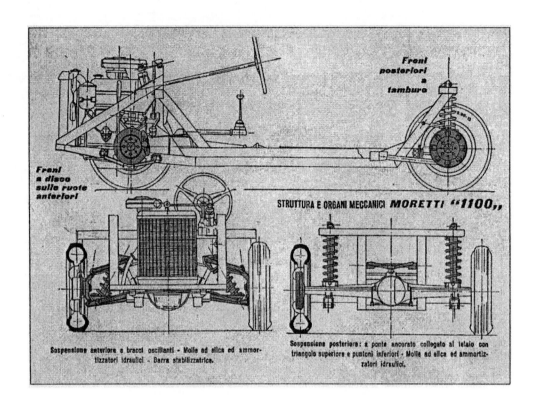

STRUTTURA E ORGANI MECCANICI *MORETTI "1100,,*

Freni posteriori a tamburo

Freni a disco sulle ruote anteriori

Sospensione anteriore a bracci oscillanti - Molle ad elica ed ammortizzatori idraulici - Barra stabilizzatrice.

Sospensione posteriore: a ponte ancorato collegato al telaio con triangolo superiore e puntoni inferiori - Molle ad elica ed ammortizzatori idraulici.

Moretti Jeep

Moretti
Racing record

Date	Event	Drivers	Car	Position
1953				
25 – 26 April	Mille Miglia	Renzo Rossi/ B. Morpurgo	Moretti 750S	174th place
		Car ran as number 2228 in the Sports Group		
1954				
1 - 2 May	Mille Miglia	Fontana/ Gino Munaro	Moretti 750 Gran Sport	Did not finish
		Car ran as number 2332 in the Sports Group		
1955				
30 April – 1 May	Mille Miglia	Gianni Balzarini/ Diascoride Lanza	Moretti 750S Spider	145th place
		Car ran as number 013 in the Sports Group		
30 April – 1 May	Mille Miglia	Lino Fayen	Moretti 750S Spider	Did not finish
		Car ran as number 043 in the Sports group		
30 April – 1 May	Mille Miglia	Nicola Larosa	Moretti 750 Gran Sport	Did not finish
		Car ran as number 012 in the Sports Group		
30 April – 1 May	Mille Miglia	Giorgio Ubezzi	Moretti 750	Did not finish
		Car ran as number 017 in the Sports Group		
30 April – 1 May	Mille Miglia	Mario Recchi	Moretti 750S	Did not finish
		Car ran as number 035 in the Sports Group		
1956				
28 – 29 April	Mille Miglia	Agostino Gariboldi	Moretti 750S	159th place
		Car ran as number 212 in the Sports Group		
28 – 29 April	Mille Miglia	Ottavio Guarducci	Moretti 750	Did not finish
		Car ran as number 34 in the 750 class		
28 – 29 April	Mille Miglia	Ezio Bricarello	Moretti 750	Did not finish
		Car ran as number 36 in the 750 class		
28 – 29 April	Mille Miglia	Silvio Rossi	Moretti 750S	Did not finish
		Car ran as number 156 in the 750 class		
28 – 29 April	Mille Miglia	Aquilino Branca	Moretti 750S	Did not finish
		Car ran as numer 157 in the 750 class		
28 – 29 April	Mille Miglia	Luigi Bettiol	Moretti 750S	Did not finish
		Car ran as number 159 in the 750 class		
28 – 29 April	Mille Miglia	Azzurro Manzini	Moretti 750S	Did not finish
		Car ran as number 207 in the 750 class		

Moretti
Racing record

Date	Event	Drivers	Car	Position
28 – 29 July	Le Mans 24hr	Marcel Lauga/ Jean-Michel Durif	Moretti 750 Zagato	Did not finish
		Car ran as number 48 and completed 62 laps		
28 – 29 July	Le Mans 24hr	Marceau Escules/ Francis Guillard	Moretti 750 Gran Sport	Did not finish
		Car ran as number 47 and completed 22 laps		

1957

Date	Event	Drivers	Car	Position
11 – 12 May	Mille Miglia	Agostino Gariboldi	Moretti	Did not finish
		Car ran as number 328 in the Sports Group		

Stanguellini

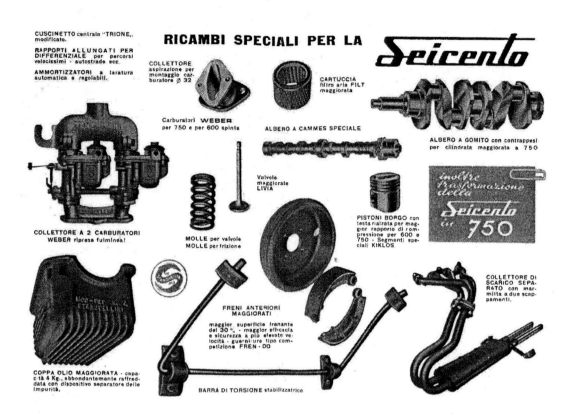

CUSCINETTO centrale "TRIONE" modificato.

RAPPORTI ALLUNGATI PER DIFFERENZIALE per percorsi velocissimi - autostrade ecc.

AMMORTIZZATORI a taratura automatica e regolabili.

RICAMBI SPECIALI PER LA *Seicento*

COLLETTORE aspirazione per montaggio carburatore Ø 32

CARTUCCIA filtro aria FILT maggiorata

Carburatori WEBER per 750 e per 600 spinte

ALBERO A CAMMES SPECIALE

ALBERO A GOMITO con contrappesi per cilindrata maggiorata a 750

COLLETTORE A 2 CARBURATORI WEBER ripresa fulminea!

Valvole maggiorate LIVIA

MOLLE per valvole
MOLLE per frizione

PISTONI BORGO con testa rialzata per maggior rapporto di compressione per 600 e 750 - Segmenti speciali KIKLOS

inoltre trasformazione della *Seicento* in 750

COLLETTORE DI SCARICO SEPARATO con marmitta a due scappamenti.

FRENI ANTERIORI MAGGIORATI
maggior superficie frenante del 30% - maggior efficacia e sicurezza a più elevate velocità - guarniture tipo competizione FREN-DO

COPPA OLIO MAGGIORATA - capacità 4 Kg., abbondantemente raffreddata con dispositivo separatore delle impurità.

BARRA DI TORSIONE stabilizzatrice

RICAMBI SPECIALI PER LA 1100/103 - 1100/TV - 1100/58 - 1200

COLLETTORE brevettato a 2 carburatori WEBER per 1100 - fino al mod. 1957
- tipo ripresa fulminea anche in 4° velocità
- tipo maggior potenza ad alto numero di giri

SFIATATOIO OLIO scarica i gas dalla testa del motore

MOLLE per valvole, per frizione e supporti motore

COLLETTORE entrata acqua

STANTUFFI BORGO con testa rialzata per maggior rapporto di compressione

INGRANAGGI CAMBIO per avvicinare le marce ed aumentare la velocità

MARMITTA DI SCARICO e tubo anteriore

Olio per motori spinti

CRUSCOTTO porta apparecchi per 1100 sino al mod. 1956

CRUSCOTTO porta contagiri da montare al posto del porta canna

ALBERO A CAMMES SPECIALE maggiori prestazioni ad alto regime di giri

COLLETTORE aspirazione per 1 carburatore - per 1100 sino al mod. 1957 - conferisce maggior ripresa e velocità

TERMOMETRO per acqua e manometro olio

FRENI ANTERIORI MAGGIORATI
maggiore superficie frenante del 40%
maggior efficacia e sicurezza a più elevata velocità
tamburo in lega leggera con anello interno in ghisa speciale
indeformabile fino sotto pressione
guarniture tipo competizione FREN-DO

COLLETTORE aspirazione e scarico con un carburatore WEBER Doppio corpo per 1100/58. Notevole aumento di velocità con forte riduzione di consumo

CONTAGIRI silenzioso e frenato con SUPPORTO SPINTEROGENO

COPERCHIO TESTA in alluminio con alette di raffreddamento

Additivo per olio

COPPA OLIO MAGGIORATA capacità 5 kg. abbondante raffreddamento indispensabile per una buona durata del motore

Vai, Vai, Vai!

Back in the fifties, Stanguellini was to Italy what Lotus was to the UK: a small manufacturer of exciting sports cars. Mike McCarthy and Mario Marti explain what happened

*Y*ou know those Italian kids who scream around on mopeds, 10 zillion revs and decibels, arrogant and cocky, lookit-me, lookit-me? I've found a car just like that.

It didn't strike me at first. It popped and banged a bit. Didn't feel like doing very much. The temperature gauge told me it was still cold, and I didn't want to do anything silly. Up to 4000rpm, approaching the no-go area. Into second, up to 4500rpm. The engine note took on a deeper crackle. A disappointing amount of urge, though, sort of bog-standard Spridget, from what looks like a pure sports-racer. But what else do you expect? It's only a 750.

The burly Italian sitting next to me suddenly becomes animated, flapping his hands: "Vai, vai". I point to the massive white tacho and enquire "Il massimo?". A pudgy finger dabs 8 on the dial. "Otto?". "Si, si!". "Otto?". "Si, si, si — vai, vai, vai!".

On your head be it, laddie. Drop down a gear, floor throttle. Instant pandemonium. Needle zaps around the dial, to 8, seriously raucous bellow from behind, snick the next gear, up to 8 again, engine hammering

Left: Vittorio Stanguellini stands at left of picture. Above: Fiat-based Stanguellini 500 from 1939. Below: two very rare birds, an 1100 Sport (623) and a 2800 Sport (624), Mille Miglia, 1950

Stanguellini

Above: legend has it that Enzo Ferrari designed the Stanguellini badge. Below: minimal frontal area of record breaker

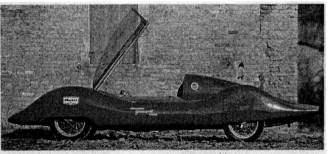

Super-streamlined Colibri record breaker — 100mph plus from 250cc

Last of Stanguellini FJs with Fiat power and Ferrari-like shark nose

Early Italy-only Formula Corsa racer with first twin-cam 750cc engine

Superb profile of little 750cc Bialbero Sport, as driven by McCarthy

Stanguellini Formula Junior, developed from Formula Corsa, was big success

Holy Mother of God, we're flying!
The little Stanguellini may only have 750cc under its bonnet, but it has the muscle of a world-class featherweight boxer. Somebody ought to tell it that this is showing off, to stay in its place, stop strutting. By all that I hold dear, I should hate it, insolent little bugger: but I fall instantly in love instead.

Stanguellini is not a very well-known name in this country. Let's face it, it's almost totally unknown. Like Giaur, Giannini, Ermini. In Italy it's another matter, but even there it's not a name on everybody's lips. Back in the fifties, it was different. It was to Italy what, say, Elva, Keift, Piper or Turner was to Britain, a small manufacturer of small sports and single-seat racers. Here, occasionally *Autosport* or *The Autocar* would have a picture and caption, or a mention in a news column of one, but that was it.

The history of the company can actually be traced back to the early days of the motor car. Francesco Stanguellini was a pioneer motorist: indeed he owned the first car in Modena, registered MO 1. He was also the Fiat agent for the area, and to this day Stanguellini is still the *numero uno* Fiat dealer in Modena. As a sideline, he ran a racing team of Mignon motorbikes, which his son Vittorio rode.

And Vittorio became head of the company in 1929 on the death of Francesco. Racing had to go, but there was still *Elaborazione e trasformazione* to enjoy. Naturally, being the biggest Fiat man in the area, the cars

Stanguellini

Above: Monti and Rugolo set off on the 1954 Mille Miglia in a 750 Sport. The start time is 11.10pm — the night before! Left: cockpit — 'air surrounded by a coating of aluminium' — is spacious

Left: gorgeous little 750cc twin-cam engine revs to 8000rpm, feels like a 2-litre

Vittorio elaborated and transformed were Fiats, and he began to earn himself something of a reputation. By 1935 a Fiat Ballila, suitably treated, was winning races. A 1500km race from Tobruk to Tripoli in North Africa in 1938 saw a Stanguellini-modified Fiat 500 win its class. So quick was the little bomb that it arrived at the finish before the officials, and ahead of all the bigger machinery which should have overtaken it. By 1940 Stanguellinis had won both the 1100cc and 750cc classes in the Mille Miglia, that year held on a triangular course near Brescia, and won overall by BMW. (This was also the event in which the first 'Ferrari', the Auto-Avia Costruzioni, appeared.) Well, there was a war on.

Getting into it is a bit like putting on a pair of jeans. Not the old-fashioned tight ones, though, but the currently fashionable loose-fit variety. The effect is even more pronounced when you're in, because the bodywork comes up to belt level.

For such a small car, there's a lotta room, but then you're surrounded mainly by fresh air with a thin coating of aluminium. You sit on red leather bucket seats, with your feet between the chassis tubing and the central tunnel, all of it in bare ally of course. You can see the little tubes that hold the body to the chassis, and the doors are also mere bits of tube covered in the ubiquitous ally. This thing is empty inside.

The gearlever is about eight to 10 inches long, topped by an enormous polished metal knob. Gear pattern is standard H, reverse

Stanguellini

across right and back. In front of you is a very thin, medium-sized, wood-rimmed, ally-spoked steering wheel with a Stanguellini badge on the boss, and behind that is a huge white Smiths tacho that shouts 'don't ignore me, baby'. There's an oil temperature gauge on the left, an oil pressure gauge on the right, and a water temperature gauge over on the far side. Assorted buttons and switches are scattered here and there. It's all very minimal.

In the post-war years, Italian motor racing blossomed instantly, far quicker than anywhere else in the world. Alfa Romeo and Maserati returned almost immediately, with that newcomer Ferrari snapping at their heels. A goodly number of the races were on public roads, or were hillclimbs, and in these events the sturdy little Stanguellinis excelled. An example: one of the 1100cc Mille Miglia cars, driven by a gent called Auricchio, won the 1946 Gran Premio di Pescara outright. In 1947, Stanguellinis won 37 races (mostly in class) out of 43 entered, to which you can add 20 seconds and 12 thirds. Which goes to show just how much racing there was, and how the diddy Modenese cars dominated their classes.

Although Vittorio had cracked the problems of tuning Fiat engines, in 1948 he extended his involvement by producing a tubular chassis, designed in co-operation with *Ingeniere* Massimino. There was independent front suspension, and these little cycle-winged *Sport Internazionale* models were, of course, Fiat-powered with Stanguellini mods.

That same year Vittorio Stanguellini discovered Weber carburettors and started fitting them to his engines: it was a two-way traffic situation as well, since he contributed to their development.

The clutch is fairly sharp, as you might expect, being of the semi-racing type and in a light car to boot. With minimal space down in the footwell you can heel and toe quite easily. The gearchange is lovely, chonk, chonk, chonk, with short throws: the faster you flick the lever, and the higher the revs, the better the change too. Oddly enough, engine response at low revs is not as instantaneous as you might expect from such a small engine: there's a fair bit of flywheel effect down there somewhere. At high revs it's another matter.

Although he was reasonably happy improving the 1100cc Fiat engines, which could by then give some 80bhp, Vittorio decided there wasn't a great deal more he could do with the 500cc Topolino unit. There was only one thing to do: make his own engine.

And it was a stunning piece of kit. With twin overhead camshafts and all-alloy construction plus, of course, Weber carbs, it punched out 60bhp at 7500rpm, enough to give his little racers a hearty performance. The result was a continuation of the stranglehold on the smaller classes in the various Italian championships. Records show that these 750 Bialbero Sports won the Campionato Italiano Sport in 1954, 1955 and 1956, and the Campionato Assoluto della Montagna in 1957.

By 1956 there was a *monoposto* Bialbero Corsa, an offset-seat, tubular-framed car

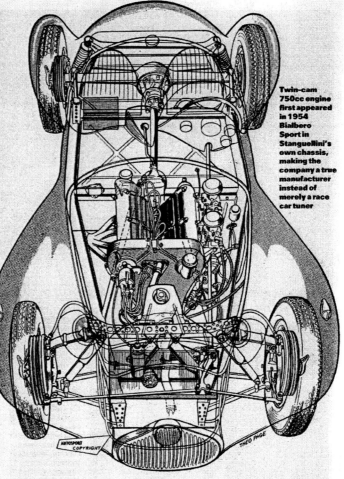

Twin-cam 750cc engine first appeared in 1954 Bialbero Sport in Stanguellini's own chassis, making the company a true manufacturer instead of merely a race car tuner

whose engine gave 92bhp which, with a weight of a mere 300kgs, gave it performance enough to take the *Campionato Italiano Formula Corsa* in 1956 and 1957.

Towards the end of the fifties interest in small sports cars waned: the loss of the Mille Miglia didn't help, since quite a few owners only used their little racers on the famous Italian 'once-a-year day'. Vittorio, though, had other interests. In 1957 Count Johnny Lurani campaigned strenuously for a new racing formula, for cars which had to use production power units to keep costs down and which would act as a training ground for up-and-coming drivers. The rules were adopted in 1958, and Formula Junior was born.

And let's face it, for a 750, it don't arf go mum. All right, put a stopwatch on it and it probably isn't all that quick, but it feels quick. Very quick. What helps here is that you sit high up, with the car around your hips, and you get blown to hell and back because the screen does nothing to protect you. On top of that you have that sharp,

deep-throated, crisp, harsh, crackly exhaust bark which sounds much more as though it belongs to a hot 2-litre. Come to that, it feels like a 2-litre.

So not a lot happens below 4000rpm, which is where it tends to pop and spit a bit: so what. It's tractable enough, if not flexible. Above that, it howls smoothly round to the magic 8. This is one sensational engine.

Being Italian-inspired, the Italians jumped at the formula and before long such legendary marques as Dagrada, Volpini, De Sanctis, Wainer, OSCA, Moretti and Bandini were battling furiously all over the continent. Also involved was, of course, Stanguellini: his *Formula Corsa* cars were almost tailor-made for the series, if you substituted Fiat 1100cc engines for the little twin overhead cam devices. As Lurani later remarked: "One emerged as an all-conquering make, the Stanguellini." Driven by the likes of von Trips, Bandini, Scarfiotti and Siffert, with arguably the best design around, it's not difficult to see why the marque was all-conquering.

Stanguellini
Racing record

Date	Event	Drivers	Car	Position
1953				
25 – 26 April	Mille Miglia	Anna Maria Peduzzi/ Franco Goldoni	Stanguellini 750 Sport	117th place
		Car ran as number 2217 in the Sports Group		
25 – 26 April	Mille Miglia	Franco Ribaldi/ C. Matteucci	Stanguellini 750 Sport	194th place
		Car ran as number 2302 in the Sports Group		
1955				
30 April – 1 May	Mille Miglia	Vincenzo Auricchio	Stanguellini 750 Sport	62nd place
		Car ran as number 026 in the Sports Group		
30 April – 1 May	Mille Miglia	Diego Bezzan/ Valentino Cocchi	Stanguellini	76th place
		Car ran as number 122 in the 1300 class		
30 April – 1 May	Mille Miglia	Anna Maria Peduzzi/ Augusto Zocca	Stanguellini 750 Sport	99th place
		Car ran as number 039 in the Sports group		
1956				
28 – 29 April	Mille Miglia	Paolo Martoglio	Stanguellini 750 Sport	128th place
		Car ran as number 143 in the Sports Group		
28 – 29 April	Mille Miglia	Philippe Faure	Stanguellini 750 Sport	130th place
		Car ran as number 143 in the Sports Group		
28 – 29 April	Mille Miglia	Roberto Lippi	Stanguellini 750 Sport	137th place
		Car ran as number 219 in the Sports Group		
28 – 29 April	Mille Miglia	F. Tinarelli/ A. Crivelli	Stanguellini-Bialbero	Did not finish
		Car ran as number 410 in the Sports Group		
28 – 29 April	Mille Miglia	Francarlo Coggi/ Daniele Agosti	Stanguellini 750 Sport	Did not finish
		Car ran as number 202 in the Sports Group		
28 – 29 April	Mille Miglia	Luigi Zannini	Stanguellini 750 Sport	Did not finish
		Car ran as number 145 in the Sports Group		

Stanguellini
Racing record

Date	Event	Drivers	Car	Position
28 – 29 April	Mille Miglia	Mario Tuccillo	Stanguellini 750 Sport	Did not finish
		Car ran as number 146 in the Sports Group		
28 – 29 April	Mille Miglia	Giorgio Cecchini	Stanguellini 750 Sport	Did not finish
		Car ran as number 211 in the Sports Group		
28 – 29 July	Le Mans 24hr	Philippe Faure/ Gilbert Foury	Stanguellini 750 Sport	Did not finish
		Car ran as number 52 and completed 36 laps		
28 – 29 July	Le Mans 24hr	Rene Duval/ Georges Guyot	Stanguellini 750 Sport	Did not finish
		Car ran as number 53 and completed 23 laps		

1957

Date	Event	Drivers	Car	Position
11 – 12 May	Mille Miglia	Francarlo Coggi	Stanguellini 750 Sport	151st place
		Car ran as number 133 in the Sports Group		
11 – 12 May	Mille Miglia	Paolo Martoglio	Stanguellini 750 Sport	Did not finish
		Car ran as number 134 in the Sports Group		
11 – 12 May	Mille Miglia	Luigi Zannini	Stanguellini 750 Sport	Did not finish
		Car ran as number 142 in the Sports Group		
11 – 12 May	Mille Miglia	Gilbert Foury	Stanguellini 750 Sport	Did not finish
		Car ran as number 145 in the Sports Group		
22 – 23 June	Le Mans 24hr	Robert Nicol/ Fernand Sigrand	Stanguellini 750 Sport	Not classified
		Car ran as number 58 and completed 214 laps		
22 – 23 June	Le Mans 24hr	Gilbert Foury/ Philippe Faure	Stanguellini Bialbero	Did not finish
		Car ran as number 56 and completed 131 laps		
22 – 23 June	Le Mans 24hr	Francesco Siracuso/ Roberto Lippi	Stanguellini 750 Sport	Did not finish
		Car ran as number 44 and completed 67 laps		

Stanguellini
Racing record

Date	Event	Drivers	Car	Position
1958				
22 March	Sebring 12hr	Carl Haas/ Alan Ross/ Charles Dietrich	Stanguellini Bialbero	21st place
		Car ran as number 53 and completed 160 laps		
21 – 22 June	Le Mans 24hr	Fernand Sigrand/ Rene Revillon/ Michel Nicol	Stanguellini 750 Sport	Not classified
		Car ran as number 53 and completed 211 laps		
21 – 22 June	Le Mans 24hr	Rene Faure/ Michel Nicol	Stanguellini 750 Sport	Did not finish
		Car ran as number 54 and completed 110 laps		
21 – 22 June	Le Mans 24hr	Georges Guyot/ Pierre Ros	Stanguellini 750 Sport	Did not finish
		Car ran as number 52 and completed 38 laps		
1959				
7 June	Nürburgring 1000km	Roger Faure/ Duvillier	Stanguellini	38th place
		Car ran as number 50 and completed 33 laps		
7 June	Nürburgring 1000km	Georges Guyot/ Roger Gourdin	Stanguellini	39th place
		Car ran as number 51 and completed 33 laps		
20 – 21 June	Le Mans 24hr	Roger Delageneste/ Paul Guiraud	Stanguellini 750 Sport	Not classified
		Car ran as number 55 and completed 220 laps		
20 – 21 June	Le Mans 24hr	Philippe Faure/ Georges Guyot	Stanguellini	Did not finish
		Car ran as number 62 and completed 58 laps		
20 – 21 June	Le Mans 24hr	Rene Revillon/ Joseph Dieu	Stanguellini 750 Sport	Did not finish
		Car ran as number 56 and completed 37 laps		